Ronald Irving read law a[...] spent his working life as a p[...] courts. He is co-author with Charles Anthony of the classic *Know Your Rights* and has written extensively on legal subjects for *The Times*.

'Ronald Irving's book is a treasure house of wit, wisdom and anecdote wholly new to me, woven together with comment and narrative drawn from his own wide practical experience and his apparently limitless erudition.'

Lord Nolan

'Few professions over the ages have come in for as much stick as the law. "The powerful exact what they can," commented Thucydides in the 5th century BC, while "the weak grant what they must."

'More recently Shakespeare remarked how "in law, what plea so tainted and corrupt but, being season'd with a gracious voice, obscures the show of evil?" And for J.B. Morton, alias Beachcomber: "Justice must not only be seen to be done, it must be seen to be believed."

'These and other choice compliments are to be found in Ronald Irving's recent collection of legal quotations, *The Law is a Ass*.'

Paul Magrath, *The Times*
Books of the Year

'The Law is a Ass'

THE CLIENT. K 1790

The lawyer / the client, by John Kay, *Kay's Portraits* II, 1838
(Mary Evans Picture Library).

'The Law is a Ass'

compiled by

Ronald Irving

Duckbacks

First published in 1999
First paperback edition 2000
Gerald Duckworth & Co. Ltd.
61 Frith Street
London W1D 3JL
Tel: 020 7434 4242
Fax: 020 7434 4420
Email: inquiries@duckworth-publishers.co.uk
www.ducknet.co.uk

Published in 2001 by Duckbacks, a paperback
imprint of Duckworth Media Group

A catalogue record for this book is available
from the British Library

ISBN 0 7156 3142 X

The royalties from this book are pledged
to Wadham College, Oxford

Typeset by Ray Davies
Printed in Great Britain by
BOOKMARQUE Ltd, Croydon, Surrey

Contents

Preface

The remark, 'I am ashamed the law is such an ass' appears in George Chapman's play *Revenge for Honour* (1654), but Charles Dickens' version in *Oliver Twist* (1838), chapter 51, is the more famous:

> 'That is no excuse', replied Mr Brownlow. 'You were present on the occasion of the destruction of these trinkets, and indeed are the more guilty of the two, in the eye of the law; for the law supposes that your wife acts under your direction.'
>
> 'If the law supposes that,' said Mr Bumble, squeezing his hat emphatically in both hands, 'the law is a ass — a idiot. If that's the eye of the law, the law is a bachelor; and the worst I wish the law is, that his eye may be opened by experience — by experience ...'.

The title was suggested by my publishers, Duckworth, after the sudden and tragic death of Colin Haycraft who had asked me to prepare a collection of legal quotations as a supplement to Duckworth's series of Sayings of specific authors: Oscar Wilde, Winston Churchill, Dr Johnson, John Keats, and so on.

My wife, who is German, kept chortling while reading the proofs. 'Germans laugh thrice at a joke,' she explained. 'First when they hear it. Next when it is explained to them, and again when they see the point.' Being a teacher of sociology, she insists I tell young people what the law is really like as a profession. When I ask colleagues whether they would choose soliciting if they had their time over again, they invariably reply, 'What else is there to do?'

The law can be great fun. Certainly it is a good training in thinking, although I did not appreciate this at the time. We had marvellous lecturers at Oxford in the 1950s — Hanbury, Jolowicz, Heuston, Waldock, and Rupert (later Lord) Cross, who was blind but kept us in fits of laughter over criminal law.

I would deny any suggestion that I chose the law because, apart from crime, it seemed the easiest way of earning a living without actually working, but I do agree that it is the best way to get experience of life at others' expense. And you meet many remarkably clever and interesting people. At the end of a successful case, C.G.L. Du Cann was invited to lunch at the Reform Club by his leader who then turned to me: 'Why don't you join us?' 'It's hardly the done thing, lunching with one's solicitor,' protested Du Cann. But his leader insisted, and so I went. Du Cann told me that he read for the bar while in the trenches during the First World War. He got leave to take the bar finals just before a big attack. 'What's the point?' asked the general, 'but let him go, if he thinks he's going to survive this war.' Like many lawyers, he was long-lived.

My most blissful memories are of sitting behind a row of barristers and silks and watching a case unfold. Although the silks have the greater prestige they are not always the brightest. The acknowledged expert on the law of evidence was the junior N.B. Cockburn. One day a dispute arose on a very abstruse point of admissibility. A senior silk rose to make his submission. The judge stopped him, smiling: 'Don't you think it would save time if we heard what Mr Cockburn thinks first?'

A colleague once mentioned that he always used Paul

Hoffman (now Lord Hoffman) as counsel if he was available. I said I had never come across him. 'Oh, he's very bright.' Months later I saw the name 'Mr Justice Hoffman' on the adjoining court door and went in. The court was deserted. Counsel in a battered wig was stumbling over a submission which he clearly had not prepared and was trying to cobble together as he went along.

The judge leaned forward sympathetically. 'Would I be right to summarise your argument in this way?' Counsel beamed as the judge in a few lucid sentences assembled an absolutely watertight argument for him. He glanced triumphantly across at his opponent. Not only was the judge completely on his side but he had conveniently done all his thinking for him. He paused for the judge to invite his opponent to attempt the impossible feat of refuting the argument.

Hoffman continued: 'Well, my answer to your submission is this …', and in even fewer sentences completely demolished his previous argument till not a shred or tatter remained.

Sometimes one sits gloomily in an almost empty court listening to another advocate holding forth most fluently and wonders how one can find anything to say at all. Suddenly the case is called, the depression lifts and one finds oneself saying things that could not possibly have been in one's mind before rising.

Rarely things go exceptionally well. I recall once waiting in court until ten minutes before one o'clock. I realised my case was hopeless but decided to make a very brief submission on the law and leave it at that. My client was a homeless man with a collection of assorted knives and tools in his knapsack. I submitted that these were the sort of items anyone might have at home. As he had no home it was reasonable that he should carry them around with him. I cited the case of the carpenter who attacked an assailant on the tube with a tool from his tool box. As I was in a hurry to finish before lunch, this all came out with remarkable clarity. My submission was rejected and my client given a nominal penalty, but immediately the court rose a voice called out from the public benches, ''Ere – I want that chap as my solicitor!' Another voice called out, 'So do I!' and I was surrounded by a mob of jubilant admirers. It has never happened since, and will certainly never happen again, but it was all very pleasant at the time.

*

My thanks go to all who have given me their help, many complete strangers. I only once met with a growl while trying to verify a source: 'I never said that. People keep throwing it back at me.'

Peter Carter-Ruck read the first part of the libel chapter, then gave me a copy of his memoirs of a life in the law. Judge Alan King-Hamilton took the trouble to telephone. 'There's a young chap on the phone pretending to be a judge,' called my wife. He was born in 1905, he told me.

Naturally I welcome comments or corrections from readers. Any contributions for a new edition, particularly in verse, will be gratefully received. Some sources are regrettably incomplete: Keats and Johnson should always be easy to trace but were not in the time available. These omissions, as Johnson said, are due to 'Ignorance, madam, sheer ignorance' (he had been rebuked for defining the pastern as the knee of the horse in his *Dictionary*).

Two excellent source books were not mentioned in the original edition of this book. Some of the best jokes were originally collected by F.R. Shapiro in his *Oxford Dictionary of American Legal Quotations* (OUP 1993), which is a treasure-house of legal wit and wisdom. So too is Gerald Warner's *Being of Sound Mind: A Book of Eccentric Wills*, from which the verse wills have been taken (Hamish Hamilton 1980).

Preface

While authors seldom acknowledge the debt due to their publishers, I thank the staff at Duckworth unreservedly and with great pleasure.

All the royalties on this book are pledged to Wadham College, Oxford.

July 2001   Ronald Irving

JUSTICE

A lawyer terrified by the apparition of Justice, *c.* 1750
(Mary Evans Picture Library).

Justice

Iustitia est constans et perpetua voluntas ius suum cuique tribuens.
(Justice is the constant and perpetual wish to render to everyone his due.)

Emperor Justinian (*c.* AD 482-565),
Institutes of the Law 1.1.1

In fact Justice means nothing more (and nothing less) than being fair. Hence the joke, which contains some truth, that a lawyer is someone who ensures that he gets what is coming to you. Even more cynical is the question: 'How much justice can you afford?'

Justice is inextricably tied up with law and order. The purpose of courts in every nation is to help keep the peace. Courts determine and punish crime. They also resolve civil disputes to prevent people taking matters into their own hands.

The biblical precept, 'An eye for an eye and a tooth for a tooth' belongs to an era that predates courts. It enjoins the injured party not to wreak vengeance beyond the injury he has suffered. In this sense it is the beginning of the idea of justice.

*

Certain principles are so fundamental that they are called the Rules of Natural Justice. First, everyone is entitled to a fair trial, that is, he must be allowed to speak in his own defence. Cicero tells us of the visit of some Eastern dignitaries to the Law Courts in Rome to hear a case of embezzlement of State funds by public officials.

'Why waste time trying the scoundrels? In our country we would have beheaded them on the spot!' exclaimed one of the party.

'That is not how we do things in Rome,' replied Cicero.

Cicero himself never received Justice. Although he had taken no part in the assassination of Julius Caesar, he was hunted down by agents of Mark Antony. Seeing that there was no escape, he thrust his head outside the curtain of his litter and was decapitated. Mark Antony himself, on his defeat by Octavius, was refused a hearing and committed suicide. As Hermann Goering pointed out at his trial, those engaged in high politics are not constrained by rules of Justice.

Rome spent a millennium developing its laws, which were finally codified by Justinian in AD 535, and the original Twelve Tables can still be cited in countries that operate under Roman law. Principles of Justice were applied at every stage in the judicial process. You cannot run an Empire without law and you cannot have an enduring legal system without Justice.

When the Roman Empire broke up, Justice toppled and her scales lay in the mire throughout the Dark Ages. The Germanic tribes that poured into Europe settled disputes by the sword. The judicial duel or 'trial by battle' was introduced into England by William the Conqueror. Eventually succeeded by due process of law and jury trial under Magna Carta, it was not actually abolished until 1819, when a rogue claimed the right and threw down the gauntlet.

*

The second Rule of Natural Justice is that the judge must be impartial. It is astonishing how frequently the latter rule has been breached, even in English courts.

One English judge who overlooked the rule was the brilliant law lord, Lord Hoffman, in the Pinochet case, when he forgot to mention his links with Amnesty International. No one for a moment believed that this had influenced his judgment that General Pinochet might stand trial in Spain, but the rule is that 'Justice must be seen to be done'. Judges must be seen to be impartial. They must have no connection whatever with any of the parties to a dispute, and in this case Amnesty was one of the parties. The case had to be reheard before a new panel of law lords.

A judge who interferes too much in the conduct of a trial may also be in breach of the rules ensuring impartiality. The late Lord Denning related how Mr Justice Hallett could never resist asking questions during his cases. As a result there were appeals against his judgments on the ground that he had 'descended into the arena' by taking too active a part in the trials in question. Although much praised by Denning for his assiduity in probing for the truth, Hallett was obliged to resign.

In the very pursuit of Justice, said Denning, our keenness may outrun our sureness and we may trip and fall. One solicitor, John Carmichael, recently recounted how an elderly lady client of his dealt with a judge who continually interrupted her evidence:

'Look, my dear, if you shut up for a moment I'll tell you what happened.'

*

In every schoolboy there is ingrained a sense of Justice. He will protest vigorously if he feels he is not being treated as well as his peers. Treating others with fairness is a principle of moral conduct as old as civilisation itself.

In ancient Egyptian mythology the god Osiris presided in the Hall of the Two Truths where the souls of the dead were weighed in the balance against the feather of truth. The feather symbolised just treatment of one's fellow men; one must not depart from Justice by even the weight of a feather. The souls of those who failed the test were devoured at once by a terrible monster.

The same test is applied in the Bible to Belshazzar before he is deposed by Xerxes. While he is feasting a mysterious hand writes upon the wall the Aramaic words: 'Mene, mene, tekel, upharsin' – 'You are weighed in the balance and found wanting.'

On the summit of the Central Criminal Court at the Old Bailey 195 feet above the ground stands the goddess Justitia upon a golden orb. She was cast in bronze and covered in gold leaf by F.W. Pomeroy ARA. In her left hand she holds the scales of Justice, in her right she brandishes her double-edged sword to punish the guilty. Contrary to popular belief she wears no blind-fold; her eyes are wide open to see that justice is done. Ironically there is no similar statue over the Royal Courts of Justice in the Strand which are known simply as the 'Law Courts'.

*

Injustice may enter the legal system at the very top, in the form of a legislature which enacts unjust laws. Or it may creep in lower down in the form of corrupt judges or officials.

Kafka's *The Trial* depicts a nightmare scenario of what happens when Justice breaks down. The protagonist, 'K', is never told what he has been arrested for. His trial is farcical and he is finally murdered in a quarry outside town. Within a few years of Kafka's death the nightmare became reality for millions under the Nazi regime. Even as he wrote, horrific injustices, torture and forced confessions were taking place in the Soviet Union, culminating in the show trials of the Stalinist era.

In *Measure for Measure* Shakespeare shows what happens when unjust laws are enforced, while in *The Merchant of Venice* he sets out the arguments for tempering the rigidity of the Common Law with principles of Equity. These plays are not just theoretical discussions but reflect the very real injustices of the time.

One particular injustice was 'pressing to death', referred to in *Measure for Measure*. Anyone who refused to plead to a charge of felony could not be tried. Instead the accused was put to *peine forte et dure*, in which great weights were piled on him to force him to plead. If he was convicted his property would pass to the Crown, whereas if he had the resolution to die without pleading it would pass to his heirs. Many resisted to the end to benefit their family. It was last invoked at the Cambridge Assizes in 1741 but was not abolished until 1772.

Shakespeare may hold the mirror up to nature, but he is careful not to refer overmuch to the injustices of current society. He never expresses disgust at torture or revulsion at public executions. Queen Elizabeth's favourite physician was hanged, drawn and quartered. Few people today have any idea of the barbarity this slow death involved. Sometimes a victim had sufficient strength left, when the executioner was burning his entrails, to sit up and strike at his tormentor.

It was routine to use torture to secure confessions. Othello proposes, in his hatred of Cassio, first to hang him, then to extract a confession. Some critics think this must be a textual error. What they do not realise is that throttling to semi-consciousness was a standard method of torture, preceding drawing and quartering.

One of the most hideous injustices of all was the persistent torture of suspected witches – who could be any woman who was old, ugly, impoverished or unpopular. They were tortured until confession and then hanged or burned. England was not alone in the persecution of women. It is estimated that about two million were killed in Europe over three centuries. The last recorded hanging for witchcraft in England was of a woman and her ten-year-old daughter in 1712. Social reform did not extend to women for several centuries. Many villages boasted a ducking stool until the late eighteenth century, and women were still being hanged for petty theft in Dickens' day.

*

As laws are laid down, the principles of justice on which they were founded crystallise and one is left with the bare bones of legal rules. This happened both in Roman Law and in the English Common Law. To temper the rigidity of the Common Law a supplementary system of law, known as Equity, was evolved, based on principles of justice and administered by the Lord Chancellor, who was dubbed 'Keeper of the King's Conscience'. Over the centuries the rules of Equity themselves also crystallised. A gulf developed between Equity and the Common Law which was not resolved until 1873 with the fusion of the two systems, when it was decreed that where there was a conflict, the rules of Equity should prevail.

Over the last hundred and thirty years the continual refinement of rules of procedure to ensure fairness in civil disputes produced a morass of regulations which became enshrined in a massive and totally unreadable tome known as the White Book. This volume was continually updated and became ever thicker as the years went by. No layman could even begin to

The last sitting of the old Court of Session, Edinburgh, by John Kay, 1808 (Mary Evans Picture Library).

understand it. Every barrister carried it when appearing in the High Court.

In April 1999, however, came the Woolf reforms. The White Book was relegated to the bin and replaced by a simplified set of rules aimed at demolishing some of the mystery and legal jargon surrounding the courts. 'Justice may be tougher but it will certainly be quicker,' remarked one leading solicitor. 'Ill-prepared cases will be put to the sword.'

What is significant for the ordinary person is that cases involving less than £5,000 will be dealt with by arbitration – you won't need a lawyer. In fact lawyers will be positively discouraged.

The Woolf reforms relate only to procedure and are neither revolutionary nor very new. Four centuries earlier, Rabelais proposed similar short-cuts to Justice. In order to speed things up he suggested getting rid of documentation entirely. Thus when Pantagruel is asked to resolve a dispute which has been dragging on interminably he declares:

'If you wish me to deal with this, first have all the papers burnt. Then have the two gentlemen come before me themselves. When I have heard them I will give my decision without any hedging.'

Rabelais wrote this as satire, but Pantagruel's words have a modern resonance. He is simply proposing that litigation be replaced by arbitration. No doubt Lord Woolf would agree with that.

The very rules and procedures laid down to ensure fair play, such as disclosing lists of documents to the other party and answering lists of questions (interrogatories), are in reality so complicated that litigation is actually slowed or impeded, if not entirely halted.

Rabelais jokes that Justice – the decision a judge will come to – is so unpredictable that the parties might as well resolve their dispute by a throw of the dice. One eminent barrister,

N.B. Cockburn, related that he actually tossed a coin to decide the division of matrimonial property in a divorce case. He pointed out that it would be quicker and cheaper, and the result would hardly differ from the point of view of fairness.

For we both alike know that into the discussion of human affairs the question of justice enters only where the pressure of necessity is equal, and that the powerful exact what they can, and the weak grant what they must.

Thucydides (fifth century BC)

How invincible is justice if it be well spoken.

Cicero (106-43 BC)

Extreme justice is extreme injustice.

Cicero (106-43 BC)

Although it be with truth that you speak evil, this also is a crime.

St John Chrysostom (*c.* 347-407),
Homilies, c. 388

To no one will we sell, to no one will we refuse or delay, right or justice.

Magna Carta (1215), article 40

Though justice be thy plea, consider this:
That in the course of justice, none of us
Should see salvation.

William Shakespeare (1564-1616),
The Merchant of Venice 4.1 (1596-7)

Portia: A pound of that same merchant's flesh is thine
    The court awards it, and the law doth give it.
Shylock: Most rightful judge!
Portia: And you must cut this flesh from off his breast;
    The law allows it, and the court awards it.

Shylock: Most learned judge! A sentence: come, prepare.
Portia: Tarry a little, there is something else.
    This bond doth give thee here no jot of blood.
    The words expressly are 'a pound of flesh'.
    Take then thy bond, take thou thy pound of flesh,
    But in the cutting it, if thou dost shed
    One drop of Christian blood, thy lands and goods
    Are by the laws of Venice confiscate
    Unto the state of Venice.

> William Shakespeare (1564-1616),
> *The Merchant of Venice* 4.1 (1596-7)

Son: And must they all be hanged that swear and lie?
Lady Macduff: Every one.
Son: Who must hang them?
Lady Macduff: Why, the honest men.
Son: Then the liars and swearers are fools: for there are liars
    and swearers enough to beat the honest men, and hang
    them up.

> William Shakespeare (1564-1616),
> *Macbeth* 4.2 (1605-6)

Plate sin with gold,
And the strong lance of justice hurtless breaks;
Arm it in rags, a pygmy's straw doth pierce it.

> William Shakespeare (1564-1616),
> *King Lear* 4.6 (1605-6)

Fresh justice is the sweetest.

> Francis Bacon (1561-1626),
> on becoming lord keeper

    Justice, while she winks at crimes
    Stumbles on innocence sometimes.

> Samuel Butler (1612-80), *Hudibras* (1663-78)

The love of justice is simply, in the majority of men, the fear of suffering injustice.

> La Rochfoucauld (1613-80),
> *Maximes* (1665)

Justice without force is powerless; force without justice is tyrannical.

> Blaise Pascal (1623-62), *Pensées* (1670)

There is no crueller tyranny than that which is perpetrated under the shield of law and in the name of justice.

> Charles Montesquieu (1689-1755),
> *De l'esprit des lois* (1748)

Justice is my being allowed to do whatever I like. Injustice is whatever prevents my doing so.

> Samuel Johnson (1709-84)

Consider what you think justice requires and decide accordingly. But never give your reasons; for your judgement will probably be right, but your reasons will certainly be wrong.

> Lord Mansfield (1705-93), advice to a newly
> appointed colonial governor who
> lacked any legal training

Where mystery begins, justice ends. It is hard to say whether the doctors of law or divinity have made the greater advance in the lucrative business of mystery.

> Edmund Burke (1729-97), *A Vindication
> of Natural Society* (1756)

The sword of the law should never fall but on those whose guilt is so apparent as to be pronounced by their friends as well as foes.

> Thomas Jefferson (1743-1826)

Justice

> This even-handed justice
> Commends th'ingredience of our poison'd chalice
> To our own lips.
>
> William Shakespeare (1564-1616),
> *Macbeth* 1.7 (1605-6)

The sword of justice has no scabbard.

Joseph de Maistre (1753-1821),
French diplomat and philosopher

The injustice done to an individual is sometimes of service to the public.

Letters of Junius (1769-71)

> For man's grim Justice goes its way,
> And will not swerve aside:
> It slays the weak, it slays the strong,
> It has a deadly stride.
>
> Oscar Wilde (1854-1900), *The Ballad of
> Reading Gaol* (1898)

Those who offend us are generally punished for the offence they give; but we so frequently miss the satisfaction of knowing that we are avenged!

Anthony Trollope (1815-82), *The Small
House at Allington* (1864)

> The rain it raineth on the just
> And also on the unjust fella,
> But chiefly on the just, because
> The unjust steals the just's umbrella.
>
> Lord Bowen (1835-94)

Justice is truth in action.

Benjamin Disraeli (1804-81), speech,
11 February 1851

Of relative justice law may know something, of expediency it knows much; with absolute justice it does not concern itself.

> Oliver Wendell Holmes, Sr (1809-94), *Pages from an Old Volume of Life* (1883)

This is a court of law, young man, not a court of justice.

> Oliver Wendell Holmes, Jr (1841-1935)

Injustice is relatively easy to bear: what stings is justice.

> H.L. Mencken (1880-1956), *Prejudices: Third Series* (1922)

Justice must not only be seen to be done. It must be seen to be believed.

> J.B. Morton ('Beachcomber') (1893-1979)

The primary duty of a lawyer engaged in public prosecution is not to convict, but to see that justice is done.

> *Canons of Professional Ethics* 5 (1908)

Mercy is not what every criminal is entitled to. What he is entitled to is justice.

> Lord Hailsham, twice Lord Chancellor (1907-)

I have a secret passion for mercy ... but justice is what keeps happening to people.

> Ross MacDonald (1915-83)

Justice is too good for some people and not good enough for the rest.

> Norman Douglas (1868-1952), *Good-bye to Western Culture*

Justice has been described as a lady who has been subject to so many miscarriages as to cast serious reflections on her virtue.

> William L. Prosser, Dean of the University of California
> Law School, *The Judicial Humorist* (1952)

Injustice anywhere is a threat to justice everywhere.

> Martin Luther King (1929-68),
> letter from jail (1963)

This court will not deny the equal protection of the law to the unwashed, unshod, unkempt and uninhibited.

> Herman Weinkrantz, New York judge, ruling that
> disapproval of hippies would not interfere with
> their civil rights, *New York Times*, 1 July 1968

For today, at least, the law [allowing] abortion stands undisturbed. For today the women of this nation still retain the liberty to control their own destinies. But the signs are evident and very ominous, and a chill wind blows.

> Harry Andrew Blackmun (1908-99), dissenting
> opinion in *Webster* v. *Reproductive Health
> Services*, 1989, in which he championed a
> woman's right to choose abortion

This is a British murder inquiry and some degree of justice must be seen to be more or less done.

> Tom Stoppard (1937-), *Jumpers* (1972)

Liberty is liberty, not equality or fairness or justice or culture, or human happiness or a quiet conscience.

> Sir Isaiah Berlin (1909-98),
> 'Two concepts of liberty' in
> *Four Essays on Liberty* (1996)

The law, as I see it, has two great objects: to preserve order and to do justice; and the two do not always coincide. Those whose training lies towards order, put certainty before justice; whereas those whose training lies towards the redress of grievances, put justice before certainty. The right solution lies in keeping the proper balance between the two.

Lord Denning (1899-1999)

The law begins by reflecting the public conscience, and the public conscience ends by reflecting the law.   Anon.

We are not accustomed to finding the word 'just' in a statute.

Judge Hilbery (1883-1965), *King's Bench Reports* vol. 2 (1938)

The expression 'just' must mean that which is right and fitting with regard to the *public interests*.

Judge Wills, *Law Times Reports* (1899)

Who thinks the Law has anything to do with Justice? It's because we have it that we can't have Justice.

William McIlvanney (1936-)

A show trial in a foreign land is not justice. It is certainly not British justice.

General Agosto Pinochet, former Chilean dictator, 7 November 1998, in response to the request of the Spanish government that he be extradited there from Britain to face charges of crimes against humanity

LAW AND ORDER

Whoever desires to found a state and give it laws, must start with assuming that all men are bad and ever ready to display their vicious nature, whenever they may find occasion for it.

Niccolo Machiavelli (1469-1527),
*Discourses upon the First Ten
Books of Livy* (1513-17)

Peace is more important than all justice; and peace was not made for the sake of justice, but justice for the sake of peace.

Martin Luther (1483-1546),
On Marriage (1530)

Order is the first requisite of liberty.

G.W.F. Hegel (1770-1831)

The only liberty I mean, is a liberty connected with order, that not only exists along with order and virtue, but which cannot exist at all without them.

Edmund Burke (1729-97), speech at
Bristol, 13 October 1774

Law and order is one of the steps taken to maintain injustice.

Andrew Bonar Law (1858-1923),
British Prime Minister

Disobedience is the worst of evils; that is what ruins a nation.

Jean Anouilh (1910-87)

Order is not pressure which is imposed on society from without, but an equilibrium which is set up from within.

José Ortega y Gasset (1883-1955),
Mirabeau and Politics (1927)

The difference between a police state and a state where the police are efficient, but democratically controlled, is a mighty thin one.

> Lord Scarman (1911-), Report on
> the Brixton Riots, 1981

The poorest man may in his cottage bid defiance to all the forces of the Crown. It may be frail – its roof may shake – the wind may blow through it – the rain may enter – but the King of England cannot enter! – all his force dare not cross the threshold of the ruined tenement.

> William Pitt, Earl of Chatham (1708-78), referring
> to the maxim that every man's home is
> his castle, in a speech *c.* 1763

There is no grievance that is a fit object of redress by mob law.

> Abraham Lincoln (1809-65), US President, address
> to the Young Men's Lyceum, Springfield,
> Illinois, 27 January 1838

Order without liberty and liberty without order are equally destructive.

> Theodore Roosevelt (1858-1919), US President,
> *The Strenuous Life* (1900)

No man is justified in doing evil on the grounds of expediency.

> Theodore Roosevelt (1858-1919), US President,
> *The Strenuous Life* (1900)

Law and order is like patriotism. Anyone who comes on strong about patriotism has got something to hide, it never fails. They always turn out to be a crook or an asshole or a traitor or something.

> Bill Maudlin, American cartoonist,
> *Loose Talk* (1980)

Law and order are always and everywhere the law and order that protect the established hierarchy.
> Herbert Marcuse (1898-1979), German-born US
> sociologist and political philosopher

Arresting a single drunk or a single vagrant who has harmed no identifiable person seems unjust, and in a sense it is. But failing to do anything about a score of drunks or a hundred vagrants may destroy an entire community.
> James Q. Wilson, Professor of Government at
> Harvard, *Time*, 11 March 1985

THE PRICE OF JUSTICE

No dough, no go.   US, Anon.

How much justice can you afford?
> Anonymous lawyer's reply to a
> client's demand for justice

Three golden rules for lawyers:
Get the money up front.
Make no promises.
Get the money up front.   US, Anon.

A lawyer with his briefcase can steal more than a hundred men with guns.
> Mario Puzo (1920-99),
> *The Godfather* (1969)

Lawyers' gowns are lined with the wilfulness of their clients.
> H.G. Bohn (1796-1884), *Handbook of Proverbs* (1855)

Always remember that when you go into an attorney's office door, you will have to pay for it, first or last.
> Anthony Trollope (1815-82), *The Last*
> *Chronicle of Barset* (1867)

Then 'tis like the breath of an unfee'd lawyer, – you gave me nothing for't.

> William Shakespeare (1564-1616),
> *King Lear* 1.4 (1605-6)

O! then, I see, Queen Mab hath been with you …
And in this state she gallops night by night
Through lovers' brains, and then they dream of love;
O'er courtiers' knees, that dream on curtsies straight,
O'er lawyers' fingers, who straight dream on fees …

> William Shakespeare (1564-1616),
> *Romeo and Juliet* 1.4 (1594-5)

You want justice, but do you want to pay for it, hm? When you go to a butcher you know you have to pay, but you people go to a judge as if you were off to a funeral supper.

> Bertolt Brecht (1898-1956), *The Caucasian Chalk Circle* (1949)

A lawyer starts life by giving $500 worth of law for $5, and ends by giving $5 worth for $500.

> Attributed to Benjamin H. Brewster

Litigant, *n.* A person about to give up his skin for the hope of retaining his bones.

> Ambrose Bierce (1842-1914), *The Devil's Dictionary* (1911)

I wanted to make it a law that only those lawyers and attorneys should receive fees who had won their cases. How much litigation would have been prevented by such a measure!

> Napoleon Bonaparte
> (1769-1821)

Justice

Once (says an author, when I need not say),
Two travellers found an oyster in their way:
Both fierce, both hungry, the dispute grew strong,
While, scale in hand, dame Justice passed along.
Before her each with clamour plead the laws,
Explain'd the matter, and would win the cause.
Dame Justice, weighing long the doubtful right,
Takes, opens, swallows it before their sight.
The cause of strife removed so rarely well,
'There take (says Justice), take ye each a shell.
We thrive at Westminster, on fools like you:
'Twas a fat oyster – live in peace. Adieu!'

Alexander Pope (1688-1744)

'Before I take your case,' said the counsellor, 'you'll have to give me a $50 retainer.'

'All right, here's the $50,' agreed Nyman, handing over the money.

'Thank you,' the lawyer said. 'This entitles you to two questions.'

'What! Fifty dollars for just two questions! Isn't that awfully high?'

'Yes, I suppose it is,' said the lawyer. 'Now what's your second question?'

Larry Wilde (1928-), The Official
Lawyers Joke Book (1982)

Law's costly, tak' a pint and 'gree.

Scottish proverb

The price of justice is eternal publicity.

Arnold Bennett (1867-1931),
Things That Have Interested Me
(1921-25)

When there's a rift in the lute, the business of a lawyer is to widen the rift and gather the loot.

> Arthur Garfield Hays (1881-1954),
> US lawyer

For many middle income people, using a lawyer is like going to the dentist. They only go because they have to, because the costs of legal services prevent their using lawyers for preventive services.

> Philip J. Murphy, *New York Times*,
> 18 January 1976

First, I charge a retainer; then I charge a reminder; next I charge a refresher; and then I charge a finisher.

> Judah P. Benjamin (1811-84), US senator and
> Confederate Secretary of War

The bar often seems designed more to maintain full employment for lawyers than to meet the needs of clients.

> Sir David Napley (1915-94), President of
> the Law Society 1976-77

As a moth is drawn to the light, so is a litigant drawn to the United States. If he can only get his case into their courts, he stands to win a fortune. At no cost to himself, and at no risk of having to pay anything to the other side.

> Alfred (later Lord) Denning (1899-1999) in
> *Smith Kline & French Laboratories Ltd* v.
> *Bloch*: Court of Appeal (1982)

The line between a bank robber and a lawyer is a very thin one … the criminal attacks society head on; the lawyer is trying to set you free after you have been caught so that you can go out and steal some more. Whether he succeeds or not, he profits from your crime. The only way you can pay him is out of the money you have got away with at one time or another, everybody knows that. It isn't called his share of the loot, of course. It's called 'the fee'. But that's only because he has a licence that entitles him to do what he's doing, and you haven't.

> Willie Sutton (1901-80), bank robber,
> *Where the Money Was* (1976)

In England, justice is open to all, like the Ritz Hotel.

> Sir James Mathew (1830-1908), quoted by
> Sir Thomas Bingham, Master of the Rolls,
> in the *Independent on Sunday*, 1994

The one great principle of English law is to make business for itself.

> Charles Dickens (1812-70),
> *Bleak House* (1852-3)

> All thieves who could my fees afford
> Relied on my orations,
> And many a burglar I've restored
> To his friends and relations.

> W.S. Gilbert (1836-1911),
> *Trial by Jury* (1875)

That whether you're an honest man or whether you're a thief,
Depends on whose solicitor has given me my brief.

> W.S. Gilbert (1836-1911),
> *Utopia Limited* (1893)

I took silver because I could not get gold; but I took every farthing that he had, and I hope you do not call that disgracing the profession.

> Serjeant Davy, 1766, on being rebuked
> for accepting silver from a client
> instead of gold

There is far too much law for those who can afford it and far too little for those who cannot.

> Derek C. Bok (1930-), President of Harvard,
> 'A Flawed System', *Harvard Magazine*,
> May-June 1983

Legal fees are outrageous. With the cost of litigation these days, I think clients would be better off if they just met in the halls and threw dice. Certainly it would be cheaper.

> Walter McLauchlin, Chief Justice, Supreme Court of
> Massachusetts, reported in *Time*, 27 July 1981

THE LAW'S DELAYS

Lawyers generally prefer not to rush things.

> Justice Kirby, Australian Law
> Reform Commission (1982)

An incompetent attorney can delay a trial for years or months. A competent attorney can delay one even longer.

> Evelle J. Younger, Attorney General of California,
> *Los Angeles Times*, 3 March 1971

Justice delayed is not only justice denied – it is also justice circumvented, justice mocked and the system of justice undermined.

> Richard M. Nixon (1913-94), *New York Times*,
> 12 March 1971

It is one of the judicial arts to manipulate time in the interest of an eventual accord.

> R.E. Ball, Chancery Master, arguing
> that delay may be beneficial

My Lord; my clients have great reason to complain of the great injury suffered by them in consequence of these causes not keeping their situation at the head of your lordship's paper, agreeably to your lordship's order repeatedly given in my hearing. It is now nearly seven years since they have been waiting for your lordship's judgement; and upwards of two years and a half ago, they had arrived at the top of the paper; at which I humbly entreat they may, until you decide upon them, remain. There is a fund in Court of £10,000 and upwards, locked up until your lordship decides on those causes; and it is therefore a matter of great importance to my unfortunate clients that your lordship's decision may not be delayed by the circumstances to which I have above alluded. It is painful to me to state to your lordship, that I have learnt from authority, which I have no reason to doubt, that the infant, for whose benefit these suits were instituted twenty years ago, died of a broken heart, on account of being kept out of his property; and that I have to contend against the bitter feelings of his relations. Under this distressing circumstance, knowing that your lordship will pardon the liberty I have taken in thus addressing you, and which nothing but the imperious necessity of the case could have induced me to have done, I have the honour etc.

> Solicitor's letter to Lord Eldon, the
> Lord Chancellor, 15 July 1820

'Reason!' exclaimed Janotus; 'we use none of that here. You wretched, worthless traitors, there isn't a more depraved bunch than you on the whole face of the earth, as I well know ...'

At these words they framed a charge against him; and he, in his turn, served them a summons. In the end the case was adjourned by the court – it is before them still – and at that point the Masters made a vow not to clean off their dirt, and

Master Janotus and his supporters vowed not to wipe their noses, until a definite judgement should be delivered.

True to their vows they have remained dirty and snotty to this day. For the court has not yet fully sifted the documents; and the judgement will be given at the next Greek Kalends, that is to say never ... These swallowers of the morning mists [judges who get up early to get the big cases] make the suits pending before them seem both infinite and immortal; and by so doing have recalled and confirmed the saying of Chilon ... that misery is the companion of lawsuits, and that those who plead in them are wretched creatures, since they come to the end of their lives long before they attain the rights they lay claim to.

François Rabelais (*c.* 1494-1553),
Gargantua (1534)

'But, my friend,' demanded Blowbroth, 'in what way do you determine the degree of obscurity of the claims put forward by the litigants?'

'As you other gentlemen do,' replied Bridlegoose, 'that is to say by the number of bags [of documents] brought in by either party. And then I use my little dice, as you other gentlemen do, to conform to the law. Of course I have large dice as well, fine and most proper ones, that I use, as you other gentlemen do, when the matter is more fluid; that is to say when there are fewer bundles.'

'And after that,' asked Blowbroth, 'how do you pronounce judgement, my friend?'

'As you other gentlemen do,' replied Bridlegoose. 'I pronounce in favour of the party to whom fate awards a good throw of the dice. So our laws ordain.'

'Yes, my friend,' said Blowbroth, 'but since you settle your judgements by chance and by the fall of the dice, why don't you put things to the hazard on the same day, at the precise hour when the parties at variance appear before you? Why all this further delay?'

'Like you other gentlemen, I consider that time ripens all things; with time all things come to light; time is the father of truth. That is why, like you other gentlemen, I suspend, delay, and postpone judgement, so that the case, being well ventilated, sifted, and debated, may in course of time come to its maturity, and so that the decision by dice, afterwards ensuing, may be borne more patiently by the losing party.'

François Rabelais (*c.* 1494-1553),
Pantagruel (1532)

THE LAW

The Court of Queen's Bench, from *The Graphic*, 1870
(Mary Evans Picture Library).

The Law

Many legal systems attempt to distil and simplify the mass of law produced over the centuries by condensing it into a code. The most famous ancient code is that of Hammurabi, king of Babylon, around 1800 BC, but it is not the oldest. Tablets have been found in Syria in the ancient city of Ebla which reveal a code going back to 2400 BC.

English law has tended to shun codification. The most brilliant attempt was made by a county court judge, Sir Mackenzie Chalmers (1847-1927), with the Sale of Goods and Partnership Acts at the end of the nineteenth century, which survive virtually unaltered.

Sir Edward du Cann, in his autobiography *Two Lives* (1995), points to the excessive accumulation of legislation as one of the obstacles to good government:

> In recent years there has been an immense growth in the volume of legislation with which parliament must deal. Fifty years ago Parliament passed into law annually 450 pages of legislation. Now it is seven times that amount, more than 3,000 pages a year. To that must be added more than 2,000 Statutory Instruments (another 10,000 pages) which can have important and far-reaching effects, plus a plethora of European material, most of which goes by unchallenged.

You can obtain a bound volume of the Public General Acts

for the last parliamentary year (some 2,500 pages) from the Stationery Office for just £275.

*

The doctrine *stare decisis* means that judges are obliged to follow the principles of law laid down in earlier cases. Thus prior court decisions are binding on subsequent judges. By reading reports of earlier similar cases a lawyer will try to gauge what view the judge will take of the facts in the case before him. This is known as the doctrine of legal precedents and its object is to introduce an element of certainty into litigation.

The idea is that a litigant should be able to ascertain his legal rights in a particular situation by looking at the way judges have ruled in the past. This desire for certainty led one US judge to declare:

'It is usually more important that a rule of justice be settled than that it be settled right.'

In his pursuit of Justice, Lord Denning argued in favour of judges' altering or modifying a legal principle when it was seen to operate unfairly or oppressively. He was often accused of acceding to the appeal of Bassanio in *The Merchant of Venice*:

> ... And I beseech you
> Wrest* once the law to your authority;
> To do a great right, do a little wrong

Portia's reply is all in favour of legal certainty and against change:

---

* 'Wrest' here means 'distort'.

> It must not be; there is no power in Venice
> Can alter a decree established.
> 'Twill be recorded for a precedent,
> And many an error by the same example
> Will rush into the state: it cannot be.

So the conflict between the need for certainty and flexibility to achieve greater justice was well known to Shakespeare. Could he have been a lawyer? The Baconians think he was Bacon dashing off plays in his spare time.

In 1959 Lord Denning, whose life spanned almost the entire twentieth century, uttered this warning in the House of Lords:

'The doctrine of precedent does not compel your lordships to follow the wrong path until you fall over the edge of the cliff.'

In practice judges have tried to resolve this perennial conflict between rigidity in the law and the need to bend the law when it is manifestly unjust. It is permitted for a judge to disregard or 'distinguish' an earlier decision of the court. He can declare that it is 'not on all fours with the facts of the present case'.

Some awkward decisions are so 'distinguished' that they are never followed at all.

*

Not surprisingly, there is little humour in the vast morass of case law. When judges indulge in facetious remarks they do not get reported but are retailed as part of an oral tradition among lawyers.

When Mr Justice Melford Stevenson imposed ten years imprisonment on an elderly recidivist, he was met with the following protest:

'My lord! Ten years! I'm seventy-six. I'll never do them.'

'Ah well,' murmured Stevenson good-naturedly, 'Do as many as you can.'

Similar asides have been attributed to Lord Justice Darling, who was something of a wag and wrote a book exposing the ironies of the law:

'If a man stays away from his wife for seven years, the law presumes the separation to have killed him; yet according to our daily experience it might well prolong his life.'

Lord Birkett, the most persuasive advocate of his generation, opined that judges' wit in legal cases was always being recycled because it was in such short supply. Someone once asked him where he had said 'The courts are open to all – like the Ritz Hotel.' He replied that he had borrowed it from Mr Justice Mathew, but that it had been attributed to Lord Bowen thirty years before and also to Lord Justice Chitty.

As to F.E. Smith's remark that he always drank a couple of pints over lunch 'to bring himself down to the level of the bench', this goes back 300 years to Sir John Millicent and has surfaced periodically ever since.

F.E. was by no means impervious to disparaging remarks, though he was seldom at a loss for a riposte. In one case his legal skill was unfairly criticised by Mr Justice Ridley who said, as Smith was rising to address the jury:

'Well, Mr Smith, I have read the pleadings and I do not think much of your case.'

Smith remained unperturbed: 'Indeed, my lord, I'm sorry to hear that, but your Lordship will find that the more you hear of it, the more it will grow on you.'

*

F.E. Smith's rejoinder must have crossed the Atlantic, for the witticism reappeared in the Marx Brothers' film *A Night at the Opera* (1935). Groucho presents Chico (who cannot read) with a contract which he proceeds to read to him:

Groucho: 'The party of the first part shall be known in this contract as the party of the first part.' How do you like that? pretty neat, eh?

Chico: No, that'sa no good.

Groucho: What's the matter with it?

Chico: I don't know. Let's hear it again.

Groucho: 'The party of the first part shall be known in this contract as the party of the first part.'

Chico: It sounds a little better this time.

Groucho: Well, it grows on you. Want to hear some more?

Chico: Only the first part.

They go through the contract tearing off clauses as Chico expresses disapproval until only one clause remains. Chico demands to know what it says.

Groucho: Oh, that's nothing. That's the usual clause in every contract. It says that if any of the parties participating in the contract are shown to be not in their right mind, the contract is nullified.

Chico: What do you call it?

Groucho: That's what they call a sanity clause.

Chico: You can't fool me. There ain't no sanity clause!

Even A.P. Herbert never succeeded so triumphantly in ridiculing legal claptrap.

The most brilliant modern parody of legal gobble-de-gook comes from the pen of the American humorist Bill Bryson. It first appeared in the *Mail on Sunday* in October 1997.

Bryson conjures up the bewilderment we all experience when faced with an interminable and incomprehensible legal document. Groucho and Chico dealt with their contract by steadily tearing bits off it and thus eventually destroying it. Bryson's 'How to Hire a Car' is more Kafkaesque. We share his hapless resignation to the inanity of insurance legalese as recited by a clerk at airport car-hire:

Clerk: Do you want Third Party Liability Waiver Damage Exclusion Cover?

Bryson (uncertainly): I don't know. What is it?

Clerk: It provides cover in the event of a Second Party Indemnification claim being made against you, or a First or Second Party Exclusion Claim being made against you on behalf of a fourth party twice removed.

Bryson (wretchedly): I don't understand any of this.

Clerk (impatiently): Look, suppose you crash into a person who has Second Party Disallowance Invalidity Cover but not First and Third Party Accident Indemnification. If you've got Third Party Waiver Damage Exclusion Cover you don't have to claim on your own policy under the Single Digit Reverse Liability Waiver. How much Personal Loss Rollover do you carry?

Bryson (inadequately): I don't know. Mrs Bryson deals with these things.

*

Insurance is the key to the astronomical payments ordered by courts in the USA. More than half the money paid to Paula Jones in the White House sex scandal came from an insurance policy. When President Clinton sent a cheque for $850,000 to her in January 1999 to settle her claim that he had sexually harassed her, the British realised that the US legal system was very different from our own. But that was nothing compared to a US jury's award of over $5 million to a secretary in a law firm who complained that she had been molested by one of the lawyers there.

Again, both these awards pale into insignificance compared with the massive *$26.6 million* awarded in favour of a male brewery executive by an outraged jury. He had recited the plot of a racy TV show to a female who then reported him to the company for – you've guessed it – sexual harassment. His consequent sacking by the company resulted in his claim.

Oddly enough, the law in the UK is little different from that in the USA. The contrast lies simply in matters of procedure. Juries in the UK decide the amount of damages (i.e. compensation) *only* in libel cases, whereas in the USA they have a free hand to award what they like in *all* claims for compensation including libel.

An important practical distinction between the two systems is that in the UK the loser pays all legal expenses. This is a great deterrent to people making doubtful or frivolous claims. But in practice it also stops many people from claiming their rights because they simply cannot afford a lawyer, quite apart from the risk of having to pay the other side's lawyers if they lose. To an extent, at least until recently, the Legal Aid Fund helped poor claimants. Once granted legal aid, a poor claimant was in an impregnable position since no order to pay legal costs could be made against him. This generally forced his well-heeled opponent to settle. The curtailing of legal aid has now shifted the balance back to a large extent in favour of the big companies.

In the USA the position is entirely different. There, lawyers take a percentage of the sum awarded, often fifty per cent or more. If they lose they get nothing, so there is a great incentive for them to fight hard for their client. The UK is trying to move in this direction, but so far there has been little enthusiasm for the 'No win, no fee' system.

Not surprisingly a great many law suits are started in the

USA, some 90 million a year. If you walk through New York or Los Angeles, one in three of the people you pass is likely to be involved in some form of litigation. New York, for instance, pays out about $200 million a year to people who have slipped and injured themselves on a protrusion or dip in the sidewalk.

In the UK the traditional attitude of judges has been 'Let the loss lie where it falls'. English judges are notoriously mean in awarding compensation – unless you happen to belong to the upper class. One judge who was injured in a motor accident was awarded vast damages. His fellow judge sympathised that he could no longer enjoy a game of golf.

According to Bill Bryson, Americans feel that if something untoward happens to them, someone else ought to pay. In Richmond, California, in the mid-1990s lawyers had a field day. An explosion in the local chemical works spread fumes over the city. Within hours a swarm of lawyers descended on the population and persuaded 70,000 of them to issue claims. The insurers of the plant were obliged to pay out a total of $180 million, of which the lawyers creamed off a staggering $40 million.

THE LAW

Laws are spider webs through which the big flies pass and the little ones get caught.

> Proverbial; can be traced back as
> far as Solon (638-559 BC)

Equity is that idea of justice, which contravenes the written law.

> Aristotle (384-322 BC), *Rhetoric* (*c.* 322 BC)

Even when laws have been written down, they ought not always to remain unaltered.

> Aristotle (384-322 BC), *Politics* 2.8

It is ignorance of the law rather than knowledge of it that leads to litigation.

> Cicero (106-43 BC), *De legibus* 1.6

Human law is law only by virtue of its accordance with right reason, and by this means it is clear that it flows from Eternal Law. Insofar as it deviates from right reason it is called an Unjust Law; and in such a case, it is no law at all, but rather an assertion of violence.

> St Thomas Aquinas (1225-74)

Becoming involved in a lawsuit is like being ground to bits in a slow mill; it's being roasted at a slow fire; it's being stung to death by single bees; it's being drowned by drops; it's going mad by grains.

> François Rabelais (*c.* 1494-1553),
> *Gargantua and Pantagruel* (1534)

Every law has its loophole.   Anon.

[Two grave-diggers are debating whether, in view of Ophelia's suicide, she may be buried in consecrated ground]

   1st Grave-digger: It must be *se offendendo*, it cannot be else. For here lies the point: if I drown myself wittingly it argues an act, and an act hath three branches — it is to act, to do, to perform; argal, she drowned herself wittingly. ... If the man go to this water and drown himself, it is, will he nill he, he goes. Mark you that. But if the water come to him and drown him, he drowns not himself; argal he that is not guilty of his own death shortens not his own life.

   2nd Grave-digger: But is this law?

   1st Grave-digger: Ay, marry is't. Coroner's quest law.

William Shakespeare (1564-1616),
Hamlet 5.1 (1600-1)

This is a burlesque of the legal arguments in Hales *v.* Pettit *(1560) arising from the suicide of Judge Sir James Hales who threw himself into the river at Canterbury. The grave-digger's speech parodies the decision of one of the judges:*

Sir James Hales being alive caused Sir James Hales to die: and the act of the living man was the death of the dead man. And then for this offence it is reasonable to punish the living man who committed the offence, and not the dead man.

Plowden's Law Reports, p. 262

Angelo: We must not make a scarecrow of the law
   Setting it up to fear the birds of prey,
   And let it keep one shape, till custom make it
   Their perch and not their terror.

William Shakespeare (1564-1616),
Measure for Measure 2.1 (1604-5)

Abundance of law breaks no law. Do more than the law requires, rather than leave anything undone that it does require.

Proverbial

Reason is the life of the law; nay, the common law itself is nothing else but reason ... The law ... is perfection of reason.

Sir Edward Coke (1552-1634),
First Institute (1628)

Necessity hath no law.

Oliver Cromwell (1599-1658), in a
speech in Parliament (1654)

Whosoever hath an absolute authority to interpret any written or spoken laws, it is he who is truly the law-giver to all intents and purposes and not the person who first wrote or spoke them.

Bishop Benjamin Hoadly (1676-1761),
dictum (1717)

'The glorious uncertainty of the law!'

Toast at a dinner for Lord Mansfield in
London in 1756, proposed by a
lawyer called Wilbraham

The law is a sort of hocus-pocus science, that smiles in yer face while it picks yer pockets and the glorious uncertainty of it is of mair use to the professors than the justice of it.

Charles Macklin (*c.* 1697-1797),
Love à la Mode (1759)

Bad laws are the worst sort of tyranny.

Edmund Burke (1729-97), speech at Bristol, 1780

The Law

In no country perhaps in the world is the law so general a study [as in America] ... This study renders men acute, inquisitive, dexterous, prompt in attack, ready in defence, full of resources ... they augur misgovernment at a distance, and snuff the approach of tyranny in every tainted breeze.

> Edmund Burke (1729-97), Second Speech on
> Conciliation with America, 22 March 1775

Torts are infinitely various, not limited or confined, for there is nothing in nature but may be an instrument of mischief.

> Sir Charles Pratt, 1st Earl Camden (1714-94),
> Chief Justice, later Lord Chancellor, in
> *Chapman* v. *Pickersgill* (1762)

Laws are always useful to those who possess and vexatious to those who have nothing.

> Jean Jacques Rousseau (1712-78),
> *The Social Contract* (1762)

Where law ends, there tyranny begins.

> William Pitt, Earl of Chatham (1708-78), in a speech
> in the House of Lords, 9 January 1770

Every man who comes to England is entitled to the protection of the English law, whatever oppression he may heretofore have suffered, and whatever the colour of his skin, whether it is black or whether it is white.

> Lord Mansfield (1705-93), Lord Chief Justice,
> judgement in the case of Habeas Corpus
> concerning the slave Somerset (1772)

The mass of the people have nothing to do with the laws but to obey them.

> Samuel Horsley (1733-1806), Bishop of Rochester,
> in a speech in the House of Lords (1795)

The lies and nonsense that the law is stuffed with, forms so thick a mist, that a plain man, nay, even a man of sense and learning, who is not in the trade, can neither see through it nor into it.

> Jeremy Bentham (1748-1832), *An Introduction to the Principles of Morals and Legislation* (1789)

Every law is an evil, for every law is an infraction of liberty. It is with government as with medicine, its only business is the choice of evils.

> Jeremy Bentham (1748-1832), *An Introduction to the Principles of Morals and Legislation* (1789)

> The law doth punish man or woman
> That steals the goose from off the common,
> But lets the greater felon loose,
> That steals the common from the goose.
>
> Anonymous eighteenth-century jibe at the Enclosure Acts

Study is truly the grand requisite for a lawyer. Men may be born poets, and leap from their cradle painters; nature may have made them musicians, and called on them only to exercise, and not to acquire, ability. But law is artificial. It is a human science to be learnt, not inspired.

> Daniel Webster (1782-1852), letter to James Hervey Bingham, 19 January 1806

An unpaid legislature and an unpaid magistracy are institutions essentially aristocratic — contrivances for keeping legislature and judicature exclusively in the hands of those who can afford to serve without pay.

> John Stuart Mill (1806-73), *On Liberty* (1859)

There is no presumption in this country that every person knows the law: it would be contrary to common sense and reason if it were so.

Judge Maule, in *Martindale* v. *Falkner* (1946)

No man can point to any law in the US by which slavery was originally established. Men first make slaves and then make laws.

Frederick Douglass, *alias* Frederick Augustus
Washington Bailey, former slave (1817-95),
in a speech in Washington (1889)

'In my youth,' said his father, 'I took to the law,
And argued each case with my wife;
And the muscular strength which it gave to my jaw
Has lasted the rest of my life.'

Lewis Carroll (1832-98), *Alice's Adventures*
in Wonderland (1865)

The Palace of Humbug

I dreamt I dwelt in marble halls,
And each damp thing that creeps and crawls
Went wobble-wobble on the walls.

Faint odours of departed cheese,
Blown on the dank, unwholesome breeze,
Awoke the never-ending sneeze.

Strange pictures decked the arras drear,
Strange characters of woe and fear,
The humbugs of the social sphere.

One showed a vain and noisy prig,
That shouted empty words and big

At him that nodded in a wig.

The wandering phantom broke and fled,
Straightway I saw within my head
A vision of a ghostly bed,

Where lay two worn decrepit men,
The fictions of a lawyer's pen,
Who never more might breathe again.

The serving-man of Richard Roe
Wept, inarticulate with woe:
She wept, that waited on John Doe.

'Oh rouse,' I urged, 'the waning sense
With tales of tangled evidence,
Of suit, demurrer, and defence.'

'Vain,' she replied, 'Such mockeries:
For morbid fancies, such as these,
No suits can suit, no plea can please.'

And bending o'er that man of straw,
She cried in grief and sudden awe,
Not inappropriately, 'Law!'

The well-remembered voice he knew,
He smiled, he faintly muttered, 'Sue!'
(Her very name was legal too.)

The night was fled, the dawn was nigh:
A hurricane went raving by,
And swept the Vision from mine eye.

Vanished that dim and ghostly bed,
(The hangings, tape; the tape was red:)
'Tis o'er, and Doe and Roe are dead!

Oh, yet my spirit inly crawls,
What time it shudderingly recalls
That horrid dream of marble halls!

Lewis Carroll (1832-98)

This is the grave of Mike O'Day
Who died maintaining his right of way.
His right was clear, his will was strong,
But he's just as dead as if he'd been wrong.

Anonymous epitaph

The rules which the courts appear to follow are merely prophecies of what the courts will do in fact and nothing more pretentious.

Oliver Wendell Holmes, Jr (1841-1935), US Supreme
Court Judge, The Path of the Law (1897)

A case is only an authority for what it actually decides. I entirely deny that it can be quoted for a proposition that may seem to follow logically from it. Such a mode of reasoning assumes that the law is necessarily a logical code, whereas every lawyer must acknowledge that the law is not always logical at all.

Oliver Wendell Holmes, Jr (1841-1935), US Supreme
Court Judge, The Common Law (1881), cited by
Lord Macmillan in Read v. J. Lyons (1947)

I know of no method to secure the repeal of bad or obnoxious laws so effective as their stringent execution.

General Ulysses S. Grant (1822-85), US President,
in his inaugural address, 4 March 1869

The Law

One of the greatest delusions in the world is the hope that the evils of this world can be cured by legislation.

Thomas B. Reed (1839-1902),
US lawyer and politician

The law, in its majestic equality, forbids rich and poor alike to sleep under bridges, beg in the streets or steal bread.

Anatole France (1844-1924),
Le Lys Rouge (1894)

The law of perpetuities
Is strewn with technicalities
Its crotchets and circuities
Exhaust the best mentalities

Anon.

Reform? Reform? — Why, aren't things bad enough already?

Lord Justice Astbury (1866-1939)

The law of land under the Common Law of England is a 'rubbish-heap which has been accumulating for hundreds of years, and … is … based upon feudal doctrines which no one (except professors in law schools) understands'.

Quoted with no source by Judge Riddell,
in *Miller* v. *Tippling* (1918)

A decision of the courts decided that the game of golf may be played on a Sunday, not being a game in the view of the law, but being a form of moral effort.

Stephen Leacock (1869-1944), *Why I
Refuse to Play Golf* (1923)

The law the lawyers know about
Is property and land;
But why the leaves are on the trees,

And why the winds disturb the seas,
Why honey is the food of bees, …
They do not understand.
> H.D.C. Pepler, in W.H. Davies, *Shorter Lyrics*
> *of the Twentieth Century (1900-22)* (1922)

The rule that you are to love your neighbour becomes in law, you must not injure your neighbour; and the lawyer's question, Who is my neighbour? receives a restricted reply. You must take reasonable care to avoid acts or omissions which you can reasonably foresee would be likely to injure your neighbour. Who, then, is my neighbour? The answer seems to be – persons who are so closely and directly affected by my act that I ought reasonably to have them in contemplation as being so affected when I am directing my mind to the acts or omissions which are called into question.
> Lord Atkin (1867-1944), in *Donoghue* v. *Stevenson* (1932),
> the case of the snail in the ginger beer bottle

We all know here that the law is the most powerful of schools for the imagination. No poet ever interpreted nature as freely as a lawyer interprets the truth.
> Jean Giraudoux (1882-1944), *La Guerre de Troie*
> *n'aura pas lieu* (1935)

The Lord Chief Justice of England recently said that the greater part of his judicial time was spent investigating collisions between propelled vehicles, each on its own side of the road, each sounding its horn and each stationary.
> Philip Guedalla (1889-1944), lawyer and historian

When A annoys or injures B on the pretence of saving or improving X, A is a scoundrel.
> H.L. Mencken (1880-1956), *Newspaper*
> *Days: 1899-1906* (1941)

The whole drift of our law is toward the absolute prohibition of all ideas that diverge in the slightest form from the accepted platitudes, and behind that drift of law there is a far more potent force of growing custom, and under that custom there is a natural philosophy which erects conformity into the noblest of virtues and the free functioning of personality into a capital crime against society.

> H.L. Mencken (1880-1956), quoted in
> *New York Times Magazine*,
> 9 August 1964

Adult men and women all over England sign contracts which they do not read, at the behest of canvassers whom they do not know, binding them to pay for articles which they do not want, with money which they have not got.

> Sir Gerald Hurst (1877-1957),
> *Closed Chapters* (1942)

This contract is so one-sided that I am astonished to find it written on both sides of the paper.

> Lord Evershed (1899-1966), discussing
> a standard form contract

A verbal contract isn't worth the paper it's written on.

> Attributed to Samuel Goldwyn
> (1882-1974)

'Equality before the law' is a properly cherished principle. Yet it ought not to be pushed to ridiculous limits. Merely because a court was outrageously unfair to Mr Simple in 1900 is a poor reason for being equally unfair to Mr Timid in 1947. Thus to perpetuate a markedly unjust rule seems a queer way of doing justice.

> Jerome N. Frank (1889-1957),
> *Courts on Trial* (1949)

'The truth, the whole truth and nothing but the truth' — that stupendous falsehood which every Christian witness (alone of all witnesses) is made to declare of every statement he makes in an English Court of Law.

> C.G.L. Du Cann (1890-1983), *Maxims and Paradoxes* (1952)

Convention is the least of all laws, yet the strongest and best obeyed.

> C.G.L. Du Cann (1890-1983), *Maxims and Paradoxes* (1952)

The law's final justification is in the good it does or fails to do to the society of a given place and time.

> Albert Camus (1913-60)

It is always rather a disconcerting pursuit to endeavour to find consistent principles in the statutes relating to income tax. … The only clearly discernible principle may be that of enabling the tax to be charged on the largest numbers of persons with the least exertion on the part of the officials entrusted with the duty of collecting the tax.

> Mr Justice Danckwerts (1888-1978), in *Gatehouse* v. *Vise* (1956)

The law is not an end in itself, nor does it provide ends. It is pre-eminently a means to serve what we think is right.

> Justice William J. Brennan, Jr (1906-97), *Harvard Law Review* (1986)

An English lawsuit is not a moot or a debate, but an attempt to arrive at a result on the facts before the court: broad academic arguments are quite unsuited to the processes of the English law.

> Lord Justice Harman (1894-1970), in *Duple Motor Bodies* v. *I.R.C.* (1960)

The Law

Say it with flowers!
Say it with mink!
Say it in bowers!
But never in ink!

Notice to clients in the waiting room of Harold Michelmore
& Co, solicitors, of Newton Abbot (the right to sue for
breach of promise of marriage was abolished in 1970)

If we are to extend the law it must be by the development and
application of fundamental principles. We cannot introduce
arbitrary conditions or limitations: that must be left to legislation.

Lord Reid (1890-1975), in
Myers v. *D.P.P.* (1965)

That is the beauty of the common law; it is a maze not a
motorway.

Lord Diplock (1907-85), in
Morris v. *Martin* (1966)

The creation of a new tort is now very rare and takes a long
time. It is rather like the process of canonisation. The cause is
first of all fostered by academic well-wishers and then promoted in the lower courts. Eventually, if things prosper, the
tort will be beatified by the Court of Appeal and then, probably after a long interval, it will achieve full sainthood in the
House of Lords.

Lord Devlin (1905-92), in *The Listener*, 12 December 1968

The law is not a rigid animal or a rigid profession but a
constant search for the truth ... Justices of the Supreme Court
should grow constitutionally during their terms.

Harry Andrew Blackmun (1908-99), Associate
Justice of the US Supreme Court

Every case involves people. If we forget the humanity of the litigants before us we are in trouble, no matter how great our supposed legal philosophy may be … there is another world out there, the existence of which the Court, I suspect, either chooses to ignore or fears to recognise.

> Harry Andrew Blackmun (1908-99), dissenting
> opinion from US Supreme Court decision that
> women on low incomes could not receive
> federal funding for abortions (1977)

People will sue each other over everything and nothing. In Multnomah County District Court, Portland, Oregon, a special 'dog court' was created in 1979. There was enough legal business arising out of the activities of the canine population to keep a judge occupied for one day a week.

> David Pannick QC (1956-), *Judges*, quoting
> the *American Bar Association Journal*, 1979

An *agreement subject to contract* is not a legal agreement at all. It is closely related to the *gentleman's agreement*, reported to have been defined by Mr Justice Vaisey as 'an agreement which is not an agreement, made between two persons, neither of whom is a gentleman, whereby each expects the other to be strictly bound without himself being bound at all.'

> R.E. Megarry (1910-), *A Second
> Miscellany-at-Law* (1973)

Lawyers do not take law reform seriously – there is no reason why they should. They think the law exists as the atmosphere exists, and the notion that it could be improved is too startling to entertain.

> Lord Goodman (1913-95), *Sydney
> Morning Herald*, 17 July 1982

The Law

In Germany, under the law everything is prohibited except that which is permitted. In France, everything is permitted except that which is prohibited. In the Soviet Union, everything is prohibited, including that which is permitted. And in Italy, under the law everything is permitted, especially that which is prohibited.

> Newton Minow, 'A Comparative Study of Legal Systems', *Time Magazine*, 18 March 1985

Anyone without condoms at the weekend will have to wait until Monday.

> Decision of judge against doctor who had supplied condoms when pharmacies were closed, quoted in Michael Solomon, *Pro Life*

A judge, dining out at 'The Bell',
Found a fly in his hock and raised hell.
Said the owner in Court,
When denying the tort,
'As a rule, all our flies drink Moselle.'

> I.G. Clark, Arlesey, Bedfordshire

A handsome young bastard called Ray
Was conceived on the Rue de la Paix
According to law
He can name you his ma;
But as for his pa, je ne sais.

> Anon.

Christianity is part of the Common Law of England.

> Sir Matthew Hale (1609-76), Lord Chief Justice; this doctrine was only displaced by *Bowan* v. *The Secular Society* in 1917

The Law

Law and Equity are two things which God hath joined, but which man hath put asunder.

> Charles Caleb Colton (*c.* 1780-1832),
> *Lacon* (1820)

PRECEDENTS

All bad precedents begin as justifiable measures.

> Attributed to Julius Caesar
> (102-44 BC)

In all usages and precedents, the times be considered wherein they first began; which if they were weak or ignorant, it derogateth from the authority of the usage, and leaveth it for suspect.

> Francis Bacon (1561-1626),
> *The Advancement of Learning*
> (1605)

All the sentences of precedent judges that have ever been, cannot altogether make a law contrary to natural equity.

> Thomas Hobbes (1588-1679),
> *Leviathan* (1651)

Laws, like houses, lean on one another.

> Edmund Burke (1729-97), *Tracts on*
> *the Popery Laws* (1812)

One precedent creates another. They soon accumulate and constitute law. What yesterday was fact, today is doctrine.

> *The Letters of Junius* (1769-71)

We owe it to our ancestors to preserve entire those rights, which they have delivered to our care; we owe it to our posterity, not to suffer their dearest inheritance to be destroyed.

> Junius, to the Printer of the *Public Advertiser*, 8 August 1769

Precedents are dangerous things.
> George Washington (1732-99), letter
> to Henry Lee, 31 October 1786

It is better for the subject that even faulty precedents should not be shaken than that the law should be uncertain.
> Judge Grose (1740-1812), in
> *King* v. *Thompson* (1787)

A precedent embalms a principle. The principle may be right or may be wrong – that is a question for discussion; but at the first glance it is right to conclude that it is a principle that has been acted upon and recognised by those who preceded us.
> Benjamin Disraeli (1804-81), House
> of Commons, 22 February 1848

I believe that *obiter dicta*, like the proverbial chickens of destiny, come home to roost sooner or later in a very uncomfortable way to the Judges who have uttered them, and are a great source of embarrassment in future cases.
> Lord Justice Bowen (1835-94), in *Cooke* v. *New River*
> *Company* (1888) (*obiter dicta* are observations
> on the law made by a judge which are not
> strictly part of the legal decision)

A case is only an authority for what it actually decides.
> Lord Halsbury (1823-1921), in
> *Quinn* v. *Leatham* (1901)

Precedent, *n*. In law, a previous decision, rule or practice which, in the absence of a definite statute, has whatever force or authority a judge may choose to give it, thereby greatly simplifying his task of doing as he pleases. As there are precedents for everything, he has only to ignore those that make against his interest and accentuate those in the line of his desire. Invention of the precedent elevates the trial-at-law from the low estate of a fortuitous ordeal to the noble attitude of a dirigible arbitrament.

> Ambrose Bierce (1842-1914),
> *The Devil's Dictionary*
> (1911)

To quote me the authority of *precedents* leaves me quite unmoved. All human progress has been made by ignoring precedents. If mankind had continued to be the slave of precedent we should still be living in caves and subsisting on shellfish and wild berries.

> Philip Snowden, 1st Viscount
> (1864-1937)

When these ghosts of the past stand in the path of justice clanking their medieval chains the proper course for the judge is to pass through them undeterred.

> Lord Atkin (1867-1944), in
> *United Australia Ltd* v.
> *Barclays Bank* (1941)

In actual practice, two cases are rarely, if ever, alike ... thus a judge may have a wide discretion in deciding in a given case to follow either precedent A, or precedent B, both of which seem to have considerable bearing on this case but which, unfortunately, are completely contradictory to one another.

> Robert K. Carr (1908-79),
> *The Supreme Court and
> Judicial Review* (1942)

While Judge Cardozo pointed out with great accuracy that the power of the precedent is only 'the power of the beaten track', still the mere fact that a path is a beaten one is a persuasive reason for following it.

> Robert H. Jackson (1892-1954), in
> *Columbia Law Review* (1945)

Precedent is not all-controlling in law. There must be room for growth, since every precedent has an origin. But it is the essence of our tradition for judges, when they stand at the end of the marked way, to go forward with caution, keeping sight, so far as they are able, upon the great landmarks left behind and the direction they point ahead.

> Wiley B. Rutledge (1894-1949), *In re*
> *Yamashita* (1946), dissenting

The search for a static security – in the law or elsewhere – is misguided. The fact is that security can only be achieved through constant change, through the wise discarding of old ideas that have outlived their purpose, and through the adapting of others to current facts.

> Judge William O. Douglas (1898-1980),
> *Stare Decisis* (1949)

There is no doubt that if there were a super-Supreme Court, a substantial proportion of our reversals of state courts would also be reversed. We are not final because we are infallible; we know that we are infallible only because we are final.

> Robert H. Jackson (1892-1954), Associate Justice of
> the US Supreme Court, concurring in the ruling
> that declared the Supreme Court as the court
> of last appeal, 9 February 1953

If we never do anything which has not been done before, we shall never get anywhere. The law will stand still whilst the rest of the world goes on; and that will be bad for both.

> Lord Justice Denning (1899-1999),
> in *Packer* v. *Packer* (1954)

The law is the only profession which records its mistakes carefully, exactly as they occurred, and yet does not identify them as mistakes.

> Elliott Dunlap Smith (1891-1976), quoted in *Journal of the American Judicature Society*, June 1955

Substantive and procedural law benefits and protects landlords over tenants, creditors over debtors, lenders over borrowers, and the poor are seldom among the favoured parties.

> John Napier Turner (1929-), Attorney General of Canada, speech to Canadian Bar Association, 7 December 1969

The Common Law has not been built by judges making general pronouncements; it has been built by the rational expansion of what already exists in order to do justice to particular cases.

> Lord Reid (1890-1975)

Those terrifying verbal jungles called laws are simply such directives, accumulated, codified, and systematised through the centuries ... the decision finally rests not upon appeals to past authority, but upon what people want.

> S.I. Hayakawa (1906-), US senator

So I say it with relish. Give me a hamburger and hold the lawsuit.

> S.I. Hayakawa (1906-), address to the Senate on legal debate over which fast-food chain made the biggest hamburger, 6 October 1982

Not all precedents are good precedents, and the fact that it has been done before indicates that it is high time we stopped doing it now.

> Lord Simon (1911-), House of Lords, 21 January 1985

ON DIVORCE ...

Whoever said 'marriage is a 50-50 proposition' laid the foundation for more divorce fees than any other short sentence in our language.

> Austin Elliot, *Law Office Economics and Management*, November 1964

Zsa Zsa Gabor is an expert housekeeper. Every time she gets divorced she keeps the house.

> *Greatest One-Liners* (1970), edited by Henry Youngman

Alimony is like buying oats for a dead horse.

> Arthur 'Bugs' Bear

If there's any realistic deterrent to marriage, it's the fact that you can't afford to divorce.

> Jack Nicholson (1937-), in *Playboy*, 1972

You don't know a woman till you've met her in court.

> Norman Mailer (1923-), *Observer*, 1983

She cried and the judge wiped away her tears with my cheque book.

> Tommy Manville, American millionaire, after his thirteenth divorce

The difference between divorce and legal separation is that a legal separation gives a husband time to hide his money.

> Johnny Carson (1925-), US TV presenter

A civil annulment is obtained by about 150 couples a year. In one case a 68-year-old woman won a nullity decree on the basis that her 78-year-old arthritic husband did not fulfil her expectations of sex life.

The Times, 14 August 1999

... AND ON ANIMAL RIGHTS

If a chimp kills another chimp – or a human – in the wild, do we really want to hire a fleet of lawyers? Well, the answer to that is 'Of course we do.'

Clayton's Column, *In Brief*
magazine, March 1999

I heard from my cat's lawyer today. My cat wants twelve thousand dollars a week for Tender Vittles.

Johnny Carson (1925-), US TV presenter, on
'The Tonight Show' (1984)

FROM THE ABSURD TO THE RIDICULOUS

Gentlemen:

Last week I bought a car and didn't take your advice and have it insured. Now I want to have it insured. Will you please tell me the name of a good company which will insure it and take responsibility for the accident I had yesterday.

Letter to the Ford Motor
Company, Detroit

Gentlemen:

I had an accident yesterday. I consider that neither vehicle was to blame but if either were to blame, it was the other one.

Letter to the Aetna Casualty
Insurance Co., New York

The Law

Buick Gentlemen:
I buy your big red car yesterday, buy gallon moonshine. Take drink. Step on gas, trees and fences go by heep fast. Pretty soon see big bridge coming down road. Turn out to let bridge pass. Bang! Car gone! Gimme nother one.
Big Chief Tomochichi

Letter to the Buick Motor
Corporation, Montana,
1950s

LAWYERS

An enthusiastic junior, by Edward Tennyson Reed, *The Sketch*,
1893 (Mary Evans Picture Library).

Lawyers

In the USA there is no distinction between lawyers who specialise in court advocacy (whom we call barristers) and those who stick to their desks, now called solicitors in England. US lawyers are all known as 'attorneys'.

Until 1873 solicitors were known as attorneys-at-law, but by the nineteenth century the designation 'attorney' had become synonymous with 'crook'. Samuel Johnson's remark, reported by Boswell, reflects their low public esteem: 'He did not care to speak ill of any man behind his back, but he believed the gentleman was an *attorney*'. The Judicature Act of 1873 renamed them 'Solicitors of the Supreme Court', thus shedding the opprobrium that had formerly attended their profession.

The number of solicitors in the UK has trebled in the last 30 years, but dark clouds loom over the horizon for the current 75,000. It has been estimated that their numbers will fall by some 10,000 over the next few years.

In the USA, on the other hand, the legal profession is burgeoning. There are said to be more lawyers there than in the rest of the world put together – almost 800,000, three times as many as in 1960.

*

Please ye we may contrive this afternoon …
And do as adversaries do in law,
Strive mightily, but eat and drink as friends.
The Taming of the Shrew 1.2

Here Tranio is addressing Gremio and Hortensio – all three being rival suitors to the charming Bianca, who may not marry until her shrewish sister Kate has found a husband. 'Adversaries' here refers to opposing counsel, i.e. the barristers themselves, whereas a layman would take it as referring to the opposing parties. The allusion is to the camaraderie of barristers who often amicably lunch together during a case in which they are on opposite sides.

The other side of the coin is that there is much rivalry among lawyers generally. Barristers often feel resentment towards solicitors whom they must keep sweet in order to get briefs. Barristers may not have direct contact with the public to get work, and strictly may not even speak to a client without a solicitor being present. This rule has helped to preserve the integrity of the bar in England, since it is from the bar that judges were exclusively appointed until recent times.

The resentment felt by one barrister towards solicitors persisted even after he had reached the bench. He was asked by his clerk if he could contribute a shilling towards the funeral of a poor solicitor. 'Certainly! Here, take a guinea and bury another twenty!'

*

While there are very few cases of barristers convicted of crime, solicitors are regularly sent to prison for fraud. One judge was exceptional in finding himself in the dock at the Old Bailey in 1998 charged with involvement in mortgage fraud. Ironically, he had once been a solicitor. After some weeks the prosecution was dropped on medical grounds and he was able to retire gracefully.

In former times solicitors regarded themselves as akin to bankers of moneys deposited with them. They might borrow from these funds or lend them to other clients. In the twentieth century all this changed and now the most serious offence a solicitor can commit is to put his hand in the till. Today, lending the funds from one client's account to another client means instant striking off the roll, and is invariably followed by a term of imprisonment for embezzlement.

That is, unless you happen to be a member of the House of Lords. *The Times* recently revealed how the late Lord Goodman, a solicitor of the highest reputation, was wont to dispense largesse to various political cronies from moneys he held on behalf of his client Viscount Portman. In 1993 Portman sued Goodman for siphoning £1 million from funds Goodman had held for some 30 years on his behalf. Allowing for loss of interest and inflation, this would today amount to some £10 million.

Just before his death in 1995 Lord Goodman agreed to repay more than £500,000 but insisted on confidentiality until the year 2006. Consequently the matter never reached the ears of the disciplinary committee of the Law Society and Lord Goodman's reputation remained unsullied for the remainder of his career.

In the 1970s Ronald Shulman, a barrister, was summoned over alleged forgery of his deceased friend's will. He avoided trial by vanishing abroad and was never heard of again. This was known as the 'Penny Brahms' case after the widow of the dead man. The fake will insulted her by bequeathing her a shilling and a nude photograph of herself.

Corrupt judges are seldom punished very severely. Shakespeare makes this point satirically in *Measure for Measure*, when Judge Angelo promises Isabel that he will spare her brother's life if she will consent to sexual relations. He is only lightly reprimanded by the Duke and sentenced to marry the woman he jilted years ago because her dowry had been lost in a shipwreck.

One of England's greatest judges, Sir Francis Bacon, who rose to be Lord Chancellor, actually confessed to receiving bribes. He declared, however, that he had never allowed a bribe to influence his judgment. He was sentenced to a huge fine and imprisonment, but luck was on his side; the fine was remitted and he spent only a few days in the Tower. His legal and parliamentary career over, he married a wealthy heiress and continued to live in grand style. He was one of the most influential thinkers and writers of his generation.

One thing a judge may never do is 'dish the dirt' on fellow judges. In this respect he is bound by a code of silence stricter than the oath which binds members of the Mafia. Its breach involves a penalty more terrifying than death – judicial ostracism.

In 1941 one of our greatest judges, Lord Atkin, publicly told his fellow Law Lords that they were judicial idiots, and in a dissenting judgement in favour of individual liberty accused them of employing a system of logic more appropriate to Humpty Dumpty in *Alice Through the Looking Glass* than to members of His Majesty's judiciary.

History has since proved him right, but at the time his fellow judges were so stung by his criticism that they deliberately shunned him when he brought his daughter to lunch. Their subsequent ostracism so distressed him that he died of a broken heart three years later.

In 1985 Lord Devlin, who had retired as a judge twenty years earlier and, to the displeasure of the entire judiciary, had taken a better-paid job in the City, wrote his memoirs. He referred to Lord Dilhorne who had died in 1980 in unpleasant terms, including the rebuke that 'he did not have a grain of judicial sense'. Clearly he cannot have liked Dilhorne as a person, for he added the accusation that 'What the ordinary careerist achieves by making himself agreeable, Reggie achieved by making himself disagreeable.' He recalled that 'Reggie' (before he became Lord Dilhorne) had appeared in his court at the Old Bailey in 1957 to prosecute Dr Bodkin-Adams on charges of murdering patients, and that he bungled the case.

Devlin's fellow judges, even those who were not peers, never forgave his breach of judicial *omerta* and subjected him not only to an ostracism as severe as that inflicted upon the noble Lord Atkin years before, but also to ferocious attacks in the press. Devlin, not a man to suffer fools gladly, appears to have been unperturbed by their criticism.

He was not alone in his disapproval of Lord Dilhorne, of whose appointment as Lord Chancellor Norman St John Stevas declared despairingly, 'At last we have a wool-sack on the Woolsack.' Dilhorne's appointment was explained by one judge (who like F.E. Smith was not from a public school background) as the dying flicker of Old Etonianism. He was possibly the low-water mark of high judicial appointments, and we shall not see his like again.

*

England has produced a long line of outstanding judges. The Common Law is entirely the product of their intellects and contains some of the most elegant thinking to be found in the literature of the world. English judges outlawed slavery long before Parliament got round to it. Many even rejected the concept of witchcraft as an irrational superstition but felt obliged to hang witches because of popular demand. Their judgements were the cornerstone of an empire on which the sun never set.

David Pannick's book, *Judges* (1987), exposes the less acceptable face of the judiciary and is in consequence (though perhaps not wholly intentionally) extremely funny. Not many people know that King Alfred, for example, had forty-four judges hanged as 'homicides' for their false judgments.

In time of strife judges tend to get it in the neck. Simon de Sudbury, the Lord Chancellor, was chased by a mob in 1381 and beheaded. The next year Lord Chief Justice Cavendish was killed by a mob after being subjected to a mock trial. When James II fled the country in 1688, his crony the infamous Judge Jeffreys, by then Lord Chancellor, was captured in a tavern in Wapping after being recognised by a disgruntled litigant. He was thrown into the Tower and died there, of natural causes, the following year.

Disgruntled customers are the bane of judges. In Chicago in 1983 Judge Gentile was shot dead by an irate husband in a divorce case. But the English have equally short fuses. A couple of years before Judge Gentile met his untimely end, a man was sentenced to life imprisonment for having stabbed to death the judge who had given him Borstal training thirteen years before. As he was dragged from the dock he screamed at the judge:

'I won't forget you … I'll cut your throat when I get out.'

In 1664 a man was convicted of offering £100 to have the then Master of the Rolls done away with. In 1898 Sir Edward Parry was shot and seriously injured while on the bench in Manchester County Court. Small wonder, then, that judges in the UK still deem it wise to conceal their identity beneath a horsehair wig.

Not unnaturally, judges are sensitive to criticism and few will refrain from committing to prison for contempt anyone causing a disturbance in court. In 1631 a man who threw half a brick at a judge was ordered to be taken out and hanged in his presence. Modern judges tend to react less harshly to the odd missile aimed in their direction. Lord Denning recalled how books were thrown at the bench in the Court of Appeal but none of the judges batted an eyelid. As she marched out, their assailant, an otherwise dignified lady, commended them for 'their coolness under fire'. Lord Denning took no punitive measures against her.

In 1877 a senior judge made light of an egg being thrown at him as he was leaving court: 'I assumed it was meant for my brother judge sitting in the court next door.' Mr Justice McKenna made a similar jest about a handbag hurled in his direction by a temperamental Irish lady after he had sentenced her brother. 'I gave her the benefit of the doubt. I assumed that her target was the clerk of the court sitting beneath the throne, and not myself.'

*

Being appointed a judge is like being elected to an exclusive club. In 1915 when Stanley Owen (later Viscount) Buckmaster was appointed Lord Chancellor, the Master of the Rolls, Lord Cozens-Hardy, wrote to him:

'All His Majesty's judges are without exception members of the Athenaeum [a club in Pall Mall]. I presume you too will wish to become a member.'

One magistrate who was a member of the Garrick Club (also favoured by judges) regarded the RAC as 'slightly down market' and could not resist jibes at its members. When a particularly unsavoury tramp came before him he gave the man bail.

'My client does not want bail,' protested his solicitor. 'He is homeless.'

'That's not a problem,' retorted the magistrate. 'Lend him a tie and they'll put him up at the RAC.'

*

Wigs are a traditional part of court dress. They are made of horse-hair and last for life. Shall we see them in the new millennium? The likelihood is that wigs will be abolished for civil cases and family courts but are likely to be retained by popular demand in criminal cases.

Not only does formal garb impress the defendant but he actually expects a degree of formality which makes him feel that his case is being taken seriously. From the judge's point of view the wig provides a useful disguise as well as a degree of anonymity. One judge told Christopher Allan, whose firm Ede and Ravenscroft have been making wigs since 1689, that he stood unrecognised beside the family of a man he had just sentenced when he bought his sandwiches during the luncheon adjournment.

Christopher Allan, an expert on court attire for lawyers, says that since 1760 only bishops, judges and barristers have worn wigs. The last time a bishop wore a wig was in 1837 at the coronation of Queen Victoria.

*

Although law is still largely a masculine profession, in England a sea change is under way. Women now account for half the annual intake into the legal profession, and are on the increase as Queen's Counsel, the highest ranking barristers, of whom they now constitute about 12 per cent. However, they are still scarcely represented in the higher echelons of the judiciary. There are no women on the judicial committee of the House of Lords and there is only one in the Court of Appeal, though in 1999 a woman was appointed as President of the Family Division.

Several women solicitors who specialise in corporate law

earn very large salaries, but on average women earn less than their male colleagues. Only about 16 per cent of partners in solicitors' firms are female, and no woman has yet been elected leader of the Law Society. There is certainly room at the top for women lawyers.

THREE BARRISTERS

John Camden Neild (1780?-1852)
Miser and Millionaire Barrister

J.C. Neild was one of the great English eccentrics. Called to the bar at Lincoln's Inn in 1808, he was renowned for his knowledge of law and his love of the classics. In 1814 he succeeded to his father's estate, valued then at a quarter of a million pounds but in today's terms worth two or three hundred times that sum. Thereafter he developed into one of the greatest misers ever known, dedicating the last thirty years of his life solely to the accumulation of wealth.

An Old Etonian and graduate of Trinity College, Cambridge, Neild lived in a large house in Chelsea so meanly furnished that for some time he did not even have a bed to lie on. His shoes were patched and down-at-heel and he wore a blue swallow-tail coat with gilt buttons which he refused to have brushed because he said it spoiled the nap. He never went to the expense of buying a greatcoat and walked wherever he could.

When he visited his vast estate he always put up in the homes of his tenants whom he also expected to furnish him with food. The wife of one of his tenants, a Mrs Neale, saved his life in 1828 when he attempted to cut his throat.

After he died in 1852 his will left the whole of his estate – estimated at £1.5 million, then a colossal sum – to no less a personage than Queen Victoria. The Queen gave a pension to Mrs Neale, to whom Neild himself had never given a farthing.

Rufus Isaacs, Lord Reading (1860-1935)
From Cabin Boy to Cabinet Minister

Rufus Daniel Isaacs left school before he was fourteen. Signing articles as a ship's cabin boy at ten shillings a month, he tried to leave the ship at Rio but was caught. Later he left the family fruit trade for the Stock Exchange. He lied about his age to become a jobber but was ignominiously hammered out. His mother then insisted he read for the bar.

Completely without humour, he made not a single memorable utterance in his life. It is amazing how someone of such seemingly average competence plucked one plum appointment after another by sheer hard work. The key to his rise was his phenomenal energy and ambition. He would start work in the early hours but never worked after dinner.

His greatest asset was his fine presence and good looks. He was also lucky in his friendships, particularly with Lloyd George, who was also an outsider. In controversy he was admired for his firm but courteous manner.

He had an unerring talent to spot the point on which a case would turn, and in 1908 received £12,000 for a single brief. He appeared in some celebrated cases, though he did not always win. During cross-examination witnesses were often disarmed by his quiet tone and skill in understatement and the soft sell.

He was made Solicitor-General and then Lord Chief Justice, where he did very little apart from sentencing Roger Casement to death. Later he became chief negotiator for US war loans, and then British ambassador to Washington.

The greatest irony of his career came in 1920 with his appointment as Viceroy of India, a land he had visited 44 years earlier as cabin boy. Not only was he made Marquess of Reading (the first commoner to rise so high since the Duke of Wellington), but he also achieved the honour of being made Lord Warden of the Cinque Ports.

Sir Stafford Cripps (1889-1952)
Aristocrat, Eccentric, Vegetarian

Sir Richard Stafford Cripps was made Solicitor-General in 1930. Of aristocratic background, he had been called to the bar in 1913. His brilliant lucid brain quickly won him distinction, but his austere manner made him an easy target for jest. Lady Violet Bonham Carter joked:

'Sir Stafford has a brilliant mind – until it is made up!'

Winston Churchill could never resist the opportunity to make a jibe at Cripps' expense. On seeing him walk grandly through the smoking room at the House of Commons Churchill remarked:

'There, but for the grace of God, goes God.'

In 1946 Churchill attacked Cripps, quite unfairly, in a speech:

'Neither of his colleagues can compare with him in that acuteness or energy of mind with which he devotes himself to so many topics injurious to the strength and welfare of the state.'

Cripps, who was a strict vegetarian, found himself seated opposite Churchill at a dinner. Glancing mischievously across the table, Churchill could not help remarking to their hostess:

'I am glad I am not a herbivore: I eat what I like, I drink what I like … and he's the one to have a red nose!'

Again alluding to Cripps' vegetarianism Churchill remarked:

'Cripps produces the maximum intellectual output with the minimum working costs in fuel.'

Yet he joined Churchill in attacking the injustices of the Nazi regime. He opposed appeasement of Hitler so vehemently that he was finally expelled from the Labour Party. Coincidentally Hitler too was a vegetarian.

LAWYERS

Woe to you lawyers also! For you load men with burdens hard to bear, and you yourselves do not touch the burdens with one of your fingers.

Jesus to the Pharisees,
Luke 11.52

My suit has nothing to do with assault or battery or poisoning, but is about three goats which I complain have been stolen by my neighbour. This the judge desires to have proved to him; but you with swelling words and extravagant gestures, dilate on the battle of Cannae, the Mithridatic War and the perjuries of the insensate Carthaginians, the Syllae, the Marii and the Mucii. It is time, Postumus, to say something about my three goats.

Martial (AD *c.* 40-104), *Epigrams* 6.19,
to his representative in court

In the Peasants' Revolt of 1381 more judges and lawyers were killed than any other single class of person. When the men of Kent reached London they first burnt down the house of the Lord Chancellor, then the Temple, the home of the advocate even then for 200 years, and then broke into Newgate to free the prisoners. One disappointed chronicler described the escape of many lawyers from the flames: 'It was marvellous to see how even the most aged and infirm of them scrambled off with the agility of rats or evil spirits.'

Richard Du Cann QC (1924-94),
The Art of the Advocate (1964)

Falstaff: ... Boot, boot, master Shallow; I know the young king is sick for me. Let us take any man's horses; the laws of

79

England are at my commandment. Blessed are they that have been my friends, and woe to my lord chief justice!

Pistol: Let vultures vile seize on his lungs also!

William Shakespeare (1564-1616),
Henry IV, Part 2, 5.3 (1597-8)

Dick: The first thing we'll do, let's kill all the lawyers.

Cade: Nay, that I mean to do. Is not this a lamentable thing, that of the skin of an innocent lamb should be made parchment? That parchment, being scribbled o'er, should undo a man? Some say the bee stings: but I say 'tis the bee's wax, for I did but seal once to a thing and I was never mine own man since.

William Shakespeare (1564-1616),
Henry VI, Part 2, 4.2 (1590-1)

Hamlet: Why, may not that be the skull of a lawyer? Where be his quiddities now, his quillities, his cases, his tenures, and his tricks? Why does he suffer this mad knave now to knock him about the sconce with a dirty shovel, and will not tell him of his action of battery? Hum, this fellow might be in's time a great buyer of land, with his statutes, his recognizances, his fines, his double vouchers, his recoveries. Is this the fine of his fines and the recovery of his recoveries, to have his fine pate full of fine dirt? Will his vouchers vouch him no more of his purchases, and double ones too, than the length and breadth of a pair of indentures? The very conveyances of his lands will scarcely lie in this box, and must th'inheritor himself have no more, ha?

William Shakespeare (1564-1616),
Hamlet 5.1 (1600-1)

Lawyers

Jaques: Time travels in divers paces with divers persons …
Orlando: Who stays it still withal?
Jaques: With lawyers in the vacation; for they sleep between term and term.

William Shakespeare (1564-1616),
As You Like It 3.2 (1599)

> O that there might in England be
> A duty on hypocrisy,
> A tax on humbug, an excise
> On lawyers trading truth for lies.

Henry Luttrell (1765-1861)

'Conversation in Craven Street, Strand'

James Smith:
   At the top of the street the attorneys abound,
      And down at the bottom the barges are found:
   Fly, Honesty, fly to some safer retreat,
      For there's craft in the river, and craft in the street

Sir George Rose:
   Why should Honesty fly to a safer retreat,
      From attorneys and barges, 'od rot 'em?
   For the lawyers are *just* at the top of the street,
      And the barges are *just* at the bottom.

James Smith (1775-1839), solicitor to the Board of
Ordnance, resident of Craven Street; Sir George
Rose (1782-1872), Master in Chancery,
whose father was a barge-owner

Battledore and shuttlecock's a wery good game, when you an't the shuttlecock and two lawyers the battledores, in which case it gets too excitin' to be pleasant.

Charles Dickens (1812-70),
Pickwick Papers (1837)

Lawyers

If there were no bad people, there would be no good lawyers.
> Charles Dickens (1812-70), *The Old Curiosity Shop* (1841)

[Lawyers are] a society of men bred up from their youth in the art of proving by words multiplied for the purpose that white is black and black is white according as they are paid ...
> Jonathan Swift (1667-1745)

Lawyers are the only persons in whom ignorance of the law is not punished.
> Attributed to Jeremy Bentham (1748-1832)

When I, good friends, was called to the Bar,
I'd an appetite fresh and hearty,
But I was, as many young barristers are,
An impecunious party.
> W.S. Gilbert (1836-1911), *Trial by Jury* (1875)

Doctors are like lawyers, only lawyers just rob you, while doctors rob you and murder you as well.
> Anton Chekhov (1860-1904), *Ivanov* 1.3 (1887)

Deceive not thy physician, confessor, nor lawyer. ...
Go not for every grief to the physician, nor for every quarrel to the lawyer, nor for every thirst to the pot.
> George Herbert (1593-1633), *Jacula Prudentum* (1651)

A man without money needs no more fear a crowd of lawyers, than a crowd of pickpockets.
> William Wycherley (1640-1716), *The Plain Dealer* (1677)

It is the pest of our profession [law] that we seldom see the best side of human nature.

> Walter Scott (1771-1832),
> *Guy Mannering* (1815)

The charge is prepar'd; the lawyers are met;
The judges all rang'd (a terrible show!)

> John Gay (1685-1732),
> *The Beggar's Opera* (1728)

… There is a danger of lawyers becoming powerful as a combined body. The people should be guarded against it as it might subvert every principle of law and establish a perfect aristocracy … This order of men should be annihilated.

> Benjamin Austin (1752-1820), *Observations on
> the Pernicious Practice of the Law* (1786)

The only road to the highest stations in this country is that of the law.

> Sir William Jones (1746-94), jurist

I think we may class the lawyer in the natural history of monsters.

> John Keats (1795-1821)

There is the prostitute, one who lets out her body for hire. A dreadful thing, but are we ourselves so innocent? Do not lawyers, for instance, let out their brains for hire?

> Lord Brabazon (1884-1964), politician,
> motorist and aviator

There is a general prejudice to the effect that lawyers are more honourable than politicians but less honourable than prostitutes. That is an exaggeration.

> Alexander King, *Rich Man,
> Poor Man, Freud and Fruit*

Lawyers

The good lawyer is not the man who has an eye to every side and angle of contingency, and qualifies all his qualifications, but who throws himself on your part so heartily, that he can get you out of a scrape.

> Ralph Waldo Emerson (1803-82),
> *The Conduct of Life* (1860)

What chance has the ignorant, uncultivated liar against the educated expert? What chance have I ... against a lawyer?

> Mark Twain (1835-1910), 'On the Decay
> of the Art of Lying' (1882)

Barristers are public servants and may be called on just as a doctor may be called on to operate on a man suffering from a loathsome complaint.

> Sir Edward Marshall Hall (1858-1927)

Let lawyers decide trivial cases. If they were interpreters of the everlasting laws which rightfully bind men, that would be another thing.

> Henry David Thoreau (1817-62),
> *Journal*, 22 October 1859

There are two qualities that make for the highest success in the law – honesty and dishonesty. To get ahead you must either be so irreproachable in your conduct and elevated in your ideals that your reputation for virtue becomes your chief asset, or, on the other hand, so crooked that your very dishonesty makes you invaluable to your clients ... the crooked lawyer has got to be so crooked that everybody is afraid of him, even the judge.

> Arthur Train (1875-1945), *The Confessions
> of Artemas Quibble* (1924)

The barrister, by Kenny Meadows, *Heads of the People*, 1840
(Mary Evans Picture Library).

It would be pleasant to think that most advocates come into practice because they wish to serve their fellow men, but the likelihood is that such social zeal influences as many grave diggers as it does advocates.

> Richard Du Cann QC (1929-94), *The Art of the Advocate* (1964)

You'll find me a very conservative man in matters of the structure of the legal profession.

> Lord Hailsham (1907-)

I think all lawyers are conservative.

> Lord Gardiner (1900-90)

Most lawyers are conservative. That's what's wrong with them. They seem to have a vested interest in not changing the law.

> Lord Denning (1899-1999), *Sunday Times*, 1 August 1982

Procrastination is a sin of lawyers, trial judges, reporters, appellate judges, in brief, everyone connected with the machinery of criminal law.

> Macklin Fleming, *Los Angeles Times*, 24 July 1974

By the year 2000, there will be one million lawyers in the United States. There will be 250 million inhabitants. This means one lawyer for every 250 inhabitants.

I know it is insanitary, but you will have to share.

> Daniel White (1953-), US author

We have the heaviest concentration of lawyers on Earth — one for every five hundred Americans; three times as many as are in England, four times as many as are in West Germany, twenty-one times as many as are in Japan. We have more litigation, but I am not sure that we have more justice. No resources of talent and training in our own society, even including the medical care, are more wastefully or unfairly distributed than legal skills. Ninety percent of our lawyers serve ten percent of our people. We are over-lawyered and under-represented.

> Jimmy Carter (1924-), US President, Address to the
> Los Angeles County Bar Association, 4 May 1978

Japan boasts a total of less than 15,000 lawyers, while American universities graduate 35,000 *every year*. It would be hard to claim that these differences have no practical consequences. As the Japanese put it: 'Engineers make the pie grow larger; lawyers only decide how to carve it up.'

> Derek C. Bok (1930-), President of Harvard,
> 'A Flawed System', *Harvard Magazine*,
> May/June 1983

Our system of civil justice is, at times, a self-inflicted competitive disadvantage ... Let's ask ourselves: Does America really need 70 percent of the world's lawyers? ... Is it healthy for the economy to have 18 million new lawsuits coursing through the system annually? Is it right that people with disputes come up against staggering expense and delay?

> Dan Quayle (1947-), US Vice-President, Address to
> the American Bar Association, 13 August 1991

Anyone who believes a better day dawns when lawyers are eliminated bears the burden of explaining who will take their place. Who will protect the poor, the injured, the victims of negligence, the victims of racial discrimination and the victims of racial violence?

> John J. Curtin (1933-), Address to the American
> Bar Association, 13 August 1991

People think lawyers become sexual dullards in part because of the deadening influence of the legal texts they work with. Of course, we insiders know that precisely the opposite is true, and that legal literature is far more titillating than the uninitiated could possibly imagine …. I find that I am gripped by an urgent passion at the *bare mention* of certain sections of the Internal Revenue Code … For many of my friends, the thinly veiled eroticism of Blackstone's Commentaries has the same effect. I happen to know that among our kinkier class-mates the Model Penal Code and the Uniform Simultaneous Death Act are perennial favourites.

> Lee Christie (1959-), 'The Sexiest Profession',
> *Harvard Law Record*, 16 September 1983

I see nothing wrong in giving Robert some legal experience as Attorney General before he goes out to practise law.

> John F. Kennedy (1917-63), on his brother

If you think that you can think about a thing inextricably attached to something else without thinking of the thing which it is attached to, then you have a legal mind.

> Thomas Reed Powell (1880-1955), quoted in
> T.W. Arnold, *The Symbols of*
> *Government* (1935)

A lawyer is never comfortable with a friendly divorce, any more than a good mortician wants to finish his job and then have the patient sit up on the table.

> Jean Kerr, *Time*, 14 April 1961

The minute you read something you can't understand, you can almost be sure it was drawn up by a lawyer.

> Will Rogers (1879-1935), US comic
> actor and writer

Lawyers

I don't want a lawyer to tell me what I cannot do; I hire him to tell me how to do what I want to do.

> J. Pierpont Morgan (1837-1913), US financier

The best description of 'utter waste' would be a busload of lawyers to go over a cliff with three empty seats.

> Lamar Hunt (1932-), *San Francisco
> Examiner* (1982)

The deans of Florida's medical schools have announced that they will use lawyers instead of rats for experiments. They cited three reasons: Lawyers are more numerous; students don't become attached to them; and there are some things even rats won't do.

> Stephen M. Masterson (1948-),
> *National Law Journal*, 7 July 1986

Daniel Webster: You seem to have an excellent acquaintance with the law, sir.

The Devil: Sir, that is no fault of mine. Where I come from, we have always gotten the pick of the Bar.

> Stephen Vincent Benet (1898-1943),
> *The Devil and Daniel Webster* (1939)

If you can eat sawdust without butter, you can be a success in the law.

> Oliver Wendell Holmes, Jr
> (1841-1935)

Attorney, *n.* A person legally appointed to mismanage one's affairs which one has not himself the skill to rightly mismanage.

Lawyer, *n.* One skilled in the circumvention of the law.

Liar, *n.* A lawyer with a roving commission.

> Ambrose Bierce (1842-1914), entries from
> *The Enlarged Devil's Dictionary* (1967)

Many an American Congressman comes to Washington from a district attorney's office: you may be sure that he is seldom promoted because he has been jealous of the liberties of the citizen.

> H.L. Mencken (1880-1956),
> *Notes on Democracy* (1926)

The public regards lawyers with great distrust. They think lawyers are smarter than the average guy but use their intelligence deviously. Well, they're wrong: usually they're not smarter.

> Elbert Hubbard (1856-1915),
> *Contemplations* (1902)

I'm not an ambulance chaser. I'm usually there before the ambulance.

> Melvin Belli (1907-), US lawyer

A lawyer is someone who makes sure he gets what's coming to you.

> US, Anon.

I really went to the Bar because I thought it would be easier to go on the stage after failing at the Bar than to go to the Bar after failing on the stage.

> Lord Gardiner (1900-90)

It would be wrong to condemn all solicitors as I have obviously not met all 56,000 in England and Wales.

> Judge James Pickles (1925-),
> *Judge for Yourself* (1992)

A Protestant, if he wants aid or advice on any matter, can only go to his solicitor.

> Benjamin Disraeli (1804-1881), *Lothair* (1870)

You mentioned your name as if I should recognise it, but I assure you that, beyond the obvious facts that you are a bachelor, a solicitor, a Freemason, and an asthmatic, I know nothing whatever about you.

> Sir Arthur Conan Doyle (1859-1930),
> 'The Norwood Builder' in *The Return of Sherlock Holmes* (1905)

We must change our image. We must be seen as champions of justice, not parasites which feed on it.

> Law Society spokesman in radio interview (1988)

Despite the opportunity for solicitors now to have rights of audience in the higher courts, will there ever be parity between solicitors and barristers in the eyes of the judiciary?

At an interlocutory application at a county court before a circuit judge, I had counsel as my opponent. Mid-flow I inadvertently referred to him as 'my friend'.

His Honour interrupted me. 'Mrs Dismore', he chided, 'you are his friend. He is your learned friend.'

He may be, but I won.

> Jane Dismore of Breeze and Wyles Solicitors, Hertford,
> letter to the *Law Society Gazette*, February 1999

Law Society Enquiry Desk: Yes, madam, but why do you want a left-handed solicitor?

Enquiring Lady: All the solicitors I have consulted so far say 'On the one hand … on the other …'

> Anon.

A doctor complained to a solicitor at a cocktail party that he was always being buttonholed and asked for free advice by casual acquaintances. 'Do you find the same?' he asked of the lawyer.

'Oh yes, but it's quite easy to put a stop to it.'

'How?' asked the doctor eagerly.

'All I do is send them a bill. They never do it again.'

The two parted amicably, the doctor thanking the lawyer enthusiastically for his advice. The next day the lawyer sent him a bill.

Anon.

Quite frankly, I don't have all that many clients who call me 'sweetie'.

Frank Presland, solicitor for Sir Elton John, on being appointed as his business manager

Shailen Majithia is a professional dancer backing girl bands like the Spice Girls. But what he wants, what he really, really wants to do is become a solicitor. Obviously, there's only so much dreary celebrity and tedious dancing with beautiful women a guy can stand before letting rip among the glitz and glamour of the legal whirl.

In Brief magazine, April 1999

To Eugen F. Kerwin Associates
154 Nassau Street
New York City

Dear Mr Kerwin

My lawyer is going to get in touch with you because we need a notary.

Please don't send any old notary but come yourself; I want someone good looking.

Esthalia N.

ON THE BENCH

Four things belong to a judge: to hear courteously, to answer wisely, to consider soberly, and to decide impartially.

Socrates (470-399 BC)

A judge is unjust who hears but one side of a case, even though he decide it justly.

Seneca the Younger (4 BC - AD 65), *Medea*

Women ... serfs .. those under the age of twenty-one, open lepers, idiots, attorneys, lunatics, deaf mutes, those excommunicated by a bishop [and] criminal persons are ineligible for appointment to the bench.

Andrew Horn, *The Mirror of Justices*
(thirteenth century)

Judges ought to be more learned than witty, more reverend than plausible, and more advised than confident.

Francis Bacon (1561-1626), 'Of Judicature',
Essays LVI (1625)

Judges must beware of hard constructions and strained inferences; for there is no worse torture than the torture of laws. Specially in case of laws penal, they ought to have care, that that which was meant for terror be not turned into rigour.

Francis Bacon (1561-1626), 'Of Judicature',
Essays LVI (1625)

Look with thine ears: see how yond justice rails upon yond simple thief. Hark, in thine ear: change places; and, handy-dandy, which is the justice, which is the thief.

William Shakespeare (1564-1616),
King Lear 4.6 (1605-6)

In 1684 Robert Wright was promoted to the Bench while in a destitute state. His patron, Chief Justice Jeffreys, suggested to him that 'as you seem to be unfit for the bar or any other honest calling, I see nothing for it but that you should become a judge yourself'. Despite the opinion of Lord Chancellor Guildford that Wright was 'the most unfit person in England to be made a judge … a dunce, and no lawyer; who is not worth a groat, having spent his estate by debauched living; who is without honesty …', the King was persuaded by Jeffreys to appoint Wright to the Bench. Wright became so pronounced a favourite of James II that in 1687 he was promoted to Chief Justice, 'greatly accelerating and further-ing the Revolution' in 1688 by his decisions. In all his judicial functions he displayed himself by his 'ignorance, stupidity and immorality' to be one of 'the most sordid wretches' ever to sit on the Bench in England.

> David Pannick QC (1956-), *Judges* (1987),
> quoting Lord John Campbell, *Lives of
> the Lord Chancellors* (1868)

Oons, sir! Do you say that I am drunk? I say, sir, that I am sober as a judge …

> Henry Fielding (1707-54), *Don
> Quixote in England* (1734)

The Lord Chancellor:
> The law is the true embodiment
> Of everything that's excellent
> It has no kind of fault or flaw,
> And I, my Lords, embody the Law.

> W.S. Gilbert (1836-1911),
> *Iolanthe* (1882)

I shall no more mind you, than a hungry judge does a cause, after the clock has struck one.

> William Wycherley (1640-1716),
> *The Plain Dealer* (1677)

Words are a lawyer's tools of trade.

> Lord Denning (1899-1999)

Now I am a judge, the tension has gone but the anxiety to do right remains.

> Lord Denning (1899-1999)

The House of Lords is like heaven: you don't want to go there while there is still life in you.

> Lord Denning (1899-1999), on his
> appointment as law lord

Lord Denning is quite the nicest judge I ever met.

> Mandy Rice-Davies (1944-), model and
> night-club owner, remark during
> the 1962 Profumo Enquiry

Lord Denning's longevity could on occasion be a problem. Once, when I was arguing a case before him, I relied on an observation made by Viscount Simon when he spoke on behalf of a unanimous seven-member House of Lords in 1942. Suddenly Lord Denning, as Master of the Rolls, interrupted me: 'But I recall that Lord Simon was very sorry he said that. He told me so.'

> Lord Bingham of Cornhill (1933-), speaking as
> Lord Chief Justice at the thanksgiving service
> for Lord Denning at Westminster
> Abbey, June 1999

Judges of England have rarely been original thinkers or great jurists. Many have been craftsmen rather than creators. They have needed the stuff of morals to be supplied to them so that out of it they could fashion the law.

Lord Devlin (1905-92)

The strongest argument for judicial activism is not that it is the best method of law reform but that, as things stand, it is in a large area of the law the only method.

Lord Devlin (1905-92)

Judges have come under fire recently, being accused of – among many other failings – naivete, obstinacy, unworldliness, bias, inflexibility, self-esteem, ignorance, volubility, interruption, gossiping, pomposity, laziness, hectoring, impatience, irritability, deafness, falling asleep on the bench immediately after lunch, and haemorrhoids.

Bernard Levin (1928-), The Times,
18 July 1991

I feel like a second row forward who is suddenly pulled out of the scrum, given a whistle and asked to referee.

Mr Justice Megaw (1909-), on
his appointment to the bench

Judges should be empowered to impose death sentences in cases carrying penalties of more than fifteen years.

Judge Michael Argyle (1915-99), speech to law
students in Nottingham (for which he was
severely reprimanded by the
Lord Chancellor)

In 1986 Judge Michael Argyle told a jury trying a tax fraud case that the lack of Test Match cricket on television was 'enough to make an Orthodox Jew join the Nazi party'.

> David Pannick QC (1956-), *Judges* (1987),
> quoting the *Guardian*, 23 February 1986

Michael Argyle was ... remembered by staff at the Central Criminal Court for his daily patronage of the bookmaker's shop outside the court ...

> Obituary in *The Times*, 6 January 1999

English judges are an eccentric lot. When I had a full head of hair I wore a wig. Now I have no hair, I have dispensed with my wig.

> Lord Millett (1932-), on the suggestion that the lower
> courts should dispense with wigs as do the Law
> Lords, letter to *The Times*, 2 February 1999

Wigs are uncomfortable, scratchy, and of questionable hygienic quality, even if they no longer provide a home for a variety of tiny animals ... they are positively damaging to the image of the civil justice system.

> Sir Richard Scott, calling for the abolition of the
> wearing of wigs by judges and barristers in court

Taking silk consists of making one's head very hot in an absurdly large wig, and one's legs very cold with absurdly thin and draughty stockings.

> Sir John Simon, later Viscount
> (1873-1954)

Being a Judge is the best career in the world. One is never contradicted, one is never interrupted and one always has the last word.

> Mr Justice Vaisey (1877-1965)

A judge is not supposed to know anything about the facts of life until they have been presented in evidence, and explained to him at least three times.

Lord Chief Justice Parker (1900-72)

Sir Melford Stevenson ... is the son of a vicar; he was once a conservative candidate, and now lives in a house called Truncheons. He specialises in fierce sentences and offensive remarks, and once had to be reproved by an appeal judge for failing to put a crucial piece of pathologist's evidence to a jury; like most authoritarian judges, he is said to be personally very kind.

Anthony Sampson (1926-), The New
Anatomy of Britain (1971)

A jockey who had failed to weigh in after a race left the witness box before F.E. Smith (one of the counsel) could question him. 'Wait a minute,' said Mr Justice Darling, 'Mr Smith has not weighed in yet.'

Edward Marjoribanks, The Life of
Sir Edward Marshall Hall
(1929)

If anyone can imagine Little Tich upholding his dignity upon a point of honour in a public house, he has a very fair conception of what Mr Justice Darling looked like in warning the Press against the printing of indecent evidence. His diminutive Lordship positively glowed with judicial self-consciousness ... He felt himself bearing on his shoulders the whole fabric of public decency ... The terrors of Mr Justice Darling will not trouble the Birmingham reporters very much. No newspaper can exist except on its merits, a condition from which the Bench, happily for Mr Justice Darling, is exempt. There is not a journalist in Birmingham who has anything to learn from the impudent little man in horsehair, a microcosm of conceit and empty-headedness. ... One of Mr Justice Darling's biographers states that 'an eccentric relative left him much money'. That misguided testator spoiled a successful bus conductor. Mr Justice Darling would do well to master the duties of his own profession before undertaking the regulation of another.

> H.A. Gray, *Birmingham Daily Argus*
> (1900), was fined £100 for this
> 'splendid piece of invective'

In the 1860s, Lord Westbury asked Sir William Erle, who had recently retired from being Chief Justice of the Common Pleas, why he did not sit on the Judicial Committee of the Privy Council. Erle replied, 'Oh, because I am old and deaf and stupid.' Westbury was not convinced by this answer: 'But that's no answer at all,' he said. 'For I am old, and Williams is deaf and Colonsay is stupid and yet we make an excellent court of appeal.'

> J.B. Atlay, *The Victorian Chancellors* (1906),
> quoted by David Pannick QC (1956-),
> *Judges* (1987)

Nothing can be more fantastical than the distribution of prizes in the lottery of legal promotion.

> Lord John Campbell, *Lives of the
> Lord Chancellors* (1868)

For some judges, more distressing than public humiliation and the recording of a judicial mistake in the law reports is the error on which the judge privately and obsessively broods. The will of Sir Soulden Lawrence (a judge from 1794 to 1812) directed that his estate should pay the legal costs incurred by an unsuccessful litigant whose case Sir Soulden considered that he had badly tried some years earlier.

> David Pannick QC (1956-), *Judges* (1987)

Lawyers

We're the only branch of government that explains itself in writing every time it makes a decision.

> Byron R. White (1917-), associate
> justice, US Supreme Court

I was married by a judge: I should have asked for a jury.

> Groucho Marx (1895-1977)

Judges, as a class, display, in the matter of arranging alimony, that reckless generosity which is only found in men who are giving away someone else's cash.

> P.G. Wodehouse (1881-1975)

I don't want to know what the law is, I want to know who the judge is.

> Roy M. Cohn (1927-86), *New York
> Times Book Review*, 3 April 1988

Did you mail that cheque to the judge?

> Roy M. Cohn, aside to an aide

I wouldn't feel I had done a real day's work.

> Lord Gardiner (1900-90), later Lord Chancellor,
> on being asked why he declined
> appointment as a judge

Lord Goddard, Lord Chief Justice 1946-58, was a controversial judge and an unusual man. He was a frequent and popular guest in the Circuit Bar Mess and after dinner it was his wont to say, 'Now boys! What about a boat race?' Whereupon seventeen members of the Circuit would arrange themselves sitting with him on the floor in the formation of two eights, each with a cox, in which positions to the great detriment of sixteen pairs of trousers (including the judicial trousers whose wearer always occupied the position of Stroke of one of the 'boats'), the competing eights shuffled backwards across the floor until one of them crossed as victors the imaginary finishing line.

In court, Goddard's behaviour was even more extra-ordinary.

> David Pannick QC (1956-), *Judges* (1987), quoting
> Fenton Bresler's biography of Lord Goddard

Goddard as Lord Chief Justice ... was a calamity ... Goddard's influence on the cause of penal reform was almost unrelievedly malign.

> Bernard Levin (1928-), *The Times*, 8 June 1971

[Lord Thankerton (a Lord of Appeal) was] making himself a veritable nuisance by excessive talking. I was asked to speak to him, and did quite lately. He took it well but I hear ... that instead of being better he is worse than ever.

> Lord Dunedin in a letter to Lord
> Chancellor Hailsham (1935)

[Lord Thankerton] irritated some counsel by practising his hobby of knitting while on the bench.

> Robert Stevens, *Law and Politics* (1979)

[Mr Justice Hallett] was not a good listener, either in private or in public. He became known as the judge who talked too much.

> Lord Denning (1899-1999),
> *Due Process of Law* (1980)

One County Court judge complained that some of his colleagues had to share the same lavatory as the litigants and witnesses. Many people who have seen a judge in court do not recognise him without his wig. It is highly undesirable, in my view, that the judge standing next to a man in the lavatory should have the opportunity of hearing himself described as a 'cock-eyed old so-and-so…'.

> Henry Cecil, *nom-de-plume* of Judge
> H.C. Leon (1902-76), *The*
> *English Judge* (1970)

If I had the wings of a swallow
And the arse of a bloody great crow,
I'd fly to the top of the Crown Courts
And shit on old Laski below.

> Graffito in a Crown Court cell,
> referring to Neville J. Laski QC

I wanted to be a judge but they found out my mum and dad was married.

> Graffito in court cell

Yes, I could have been a judge but I never had the Latin, never had the Latin for the judging, I just never had sufficient of it to get through the rigorous judging exams. They're noted for their rigour. People come out staggering and saying 'My God, what a rigorous exam' – and so I became a miner instead. … I'd rather have been a judge than a miner. Being a miner, as soon as you are too old and tired and sick and stupid to do the job properly, you have to go. Well, the very opposite applies with judges.

> Peter Cook (1937-1995), 'Sitting on the Bench'
> from Roger Wilmut, *The Complete*
> *Beyond the Fringe* (1987)

IN COURT

A barrister embarrasses a dubious witness, by Edward Tennyson Reed, *The Sketch*, 1893 (Mary Evans Picture Library).

In Court

A lawyer has no business with the justice or injustice of
the cause which he undertakes, unless his client asks his
opinion, and then he is bound to give it honestly. The
justice or injustice of the cause is to be decided by the
judge.

Most lawyers agree with Samuel Johnson. When asked if they
have ever defended someone whom they knew to be guilty,
they will invariably protest that even a criminal is entitled to
be legally represented. Only if he actually tells the lawyer he
is guilty, will the lawyer be barred from assisting him in
putting forward a plea of innocence.

Of course, all this is complete hogwash. As one wag put it,
you can't make a living defending innocent people. Lawyers
are no more ignorant of the client's true character than Albert
Speer was of the criminality of Hitler. The fact is that the
advocate is on an ego trip. He needs to prove he can beat the
system. Unconsciously and often consciously he identifies
with the criminal and is gleeful when he gets off.

The oldest legal codes lay down rules for guarding against
lying in court. An Irish joke tells how a judge warned Paddy
of the Ten Commandments: 'Don't you know it's wrong to
bear false witness against your neighbour?'

'I'm not bearing false witness against my neighbour',
protested the yokel, 'I'm bearing false witness *for* him.'

The testing of a witness by cross-examination saved

Susanna when the elders accused her of adultery with a young man. Daniel asked each of the elders separately under what sort of tree it took place. Each named a different tree. Her innocence was established.

In the trial of Queen Caroline for adultery, her lawyer, Henry Brougham, used a similar method of questioning to discredit her Italian servant. He asked him a series of questions which were irrelevant to the charge. The servant realised that if he invented replies to these questions, witnesses could be called to prove his untruthfulness. Hoping to avoid the trap set by Brougham, he persistently replied 'Non mi ricordo' (I don't recall). Eventually the House of Lords realised the charge was fabricated and dismissed it.

Oddly enough, English law for centuries would not let the lawyer representing a person charged with a felony (any offence punishable by hanging) cross-examine, call witnesses or make a speech on behalf of the defendant. Moreover the defendant could not give evidence himself. The lawyer could address the court only on points of law. This situation lasted until 1836 by which time England was alone in the world in so curtailing the rights of people charged with capital offences.

In the scintillating trial scene in *The Merchant of Venice*, Shylock seeks to kill his debtor Antonio for non-payment of a loan. Portia, disguised as a man, presides as judge. Neither Shylock nor Antonio is legally represented. At first seeming to side with Shylock, Portia urges him not to enforce his legal right to kill Antonio. When Shylock refuses, she brilliantly turns the tables on him, accusing him of seeking the life of a citizen of Venice and declaring all his property forfeit.

Judges as skilful as Portia, who can avoid injustice where the law is oppressive, are rare indeed — but why is a woman cast in this male role? Well, England had a female monarch at the time who was fairly astute. Shakespeare underlines that women are intellectually often superior to their male counter-parts. He stresses their emotional superiority. Portia teaches Antonio (the Jew-baiter) that Jesus' law is to forgive the man who sought his life. Also to 'love thine enemies' instead of going out of one's way to pick quarrels with them. Women are becoming far more numerous in the law, but it has taken four centuries to turn the tide of male dominance.

From the point of view of justice, clever advocates are a nuisance. They can implant doubt where guilt seems crystal clear. The American lawyer Rufus Choate was so successful that it was said, 'He made it safe to murder. Thieves would enquire after his health before they began to steal.'

Anyone who goes into court as an advocate must learn three things: First, when to stand up; second, when to speak up; and third, when to shut up. Pupils at the bar are invariably told by their masters: 'Never ask a question in cross-examination unless you are certain what the answer will be.'

A witness in a case concerning a motor accident was asked how far away he was standing when he saw the impact.

'Twenty-two feet nine inches.'

'How can you be so sure?' asked counsel.

'Because when the cars collided I knew some damn-fool lawyer would ask me that, so I took out my tape measure and measured it.'

The most lethal question ever put to an expert witness was asked by Norman Birkett in the famous murder trial of a man who gave a tramp a lift, murdered him, and then set fire to his car to fake his own death. Birkett suggested that the brass nut on the fuel pipe had not come adrift in the fire, but had been tampered with to start the fire. The defence called an engineer to establish that in vehicle fires, the fuel pipe often came apart at the brass connection.

'What is the co-efficient of expansion of brass?' Birkett asked him.

The witness remained silent. Birkett sat down. The witness had been totally discredited and the defendant was convicted.

'What would you have said if the engineer had answered your question correctly?' Birkett's clerk asked him after the case.

'I should have ignored it as a matter of complete indifference,' replied Birkett, 'and gone on to something else.'

*

One of the most important rules an advocate must observe, when he calls a witness to give evidence for his client, is to avoid asking leading questions. A layman may think that a leading question is an important or searching question or even a loaded question, i.e. one charged with some hidden or improper implication. It is in fact none of these three. It is simply a question that prompts the answer wanted. Usually such a question may be answered with a simple Yes or No. A leading question may be put to a witness on the opposing side but it may not be put to your own witness. If accused of putting leading questions, an advocate should continue by asking simply: 'What happened next?' or 'What was said after that?'

This is quite separate from the prohibition against 'hearsay' evidence. As Charles Dickens tells us in *The Pickwick Papers*: ' "You must not tell us what the soldier, or any other man said, sir," interposed the judge; "it's not evidence." ' Of course, as a generalisation, this is nonsense and Dickens is having a bit of fun at the law's expense. Things said by or in the presence of a defendant or witness at a particular juncture can be very pertinent indeed. Strictly hearsay evidence is banned because it is based on information received from others, rather than personal knowledge.

Not infrequently a civil trial is followed by a criminal trial arising out of evidence given in the civil court. Oscar Wilde's prosecution for sodomy was brought on himself (see p. 142). More recently Jonathan Aitken was the author of his own conviction for perjury arising out of evidence he fabricated to support his earlier libel action.

The same thing happened in the Tichborne Claimant case. The civil trial was heard in the Court of Common Pleas and lasted 102 days (1871-2). The claimant (whose real name was Arthur Orton) was subjected to a cross-examination lasting a mammoth twenty-two days, which exposed his ignorance of what the real but deceased Roger Tichborne must have known.

Orton's counsel, Edward Kenealy, tried to argue that fat men (Orton weighed over twenty-six stone) are more forgetful and duller than thin men. The Lord Chief Justice interposed:

'Is there any authority for that? That a man growing fat his memory becomes impaired?'

A juror then interposed: 'There are fat men on the Jury.'

Kenealy: 'I should be able to show on the whole that lean men are the cleverest men.'

The Lord Chief Justice: 'There would be a division of opinion on that. The fat men would vote against you.'

Kenealy: 'I have only to go to the Bench of England, and I am sure I should find that the great majority are lean rather than fat men.'

The Lord Chief Justice: 'That is because they work so hard … If there are many more trials like this, we shall all become lean.'

Clearly Kenealy was grasping at straws in putting this forward as a legal submission. What he should have done was to call witnesses to say his client had a deficient memory. A man like Tichborne might have had blows to the head to which Kenealy might have attributed an impairment of memory. Perhaps Kenealy thought he could lighten the trial with a little humour. We shall never know.

The criminal trial of Orton the following year lasted even longer – 188 days. He was sentenced to fourteen years imprisonment for perjury.

Ironically, the person who insisted that Orton was her long-lost son was Richard Tichborne's mother, but all the other relatives gave evidence that he was not.

Kenealy met his Waterloo as a result of the case which, it was alleged, he conducted 'violently, aggressively and rudely'. He was disbarred for gross breaches of professional etiquette. It is said the case turned his mind. He even published a journal to support Orton's claim.

The trial can claim another historical first. The verdict was reported in the newspaper on the same day Orton was sentenced in 1874 thanks to the latest technology – the electric telegraph.

*

For O.J. Simpson, the civil trial unusually *followed* the criminal trial. He was acquitted of the murder of his former wife and her man friend in a sensational trial that lasted from January to October 1995 and was watched on TV by an average of 5.5 million viewers daily. But his deceased wife's parents went on to win a civil claim for huge damages against him for the unlawful killing of their daughter. Ironically the lawyers in his defence team fell out with one another over the tactics used and there was much ill feeling even though they had been on the same side.

F.E. Smith, Lord Birkenhead (1872–1930)

The son of a Birkenhead estate agent who, despite his alcoholism, qualified as a barrister and became mayor, Frederick Edwin Smith was educated at the local grammar school whence he won a classics scholarship to Wadham College, Oxford.

During his final term he lay by the banks of the River Cherwell with a book on land law unopened beside him. His senior tutor happened to pass and rebuked him for his indolence. Smith replied that English land law was a lot of nonsense and he would change it when he became Chancellor. This he achieved in 1919. But his overbearing self confidence made him many enemies. His appointment to the woolsack was described by the *Morning Post* as 'carrying a joke too far'. He was only 46, but soon came to regret having accepted such a tempting bauble. He was to become Baron, Viscount and Earl in quick succession, but as an active and energetic man, he hated the sedentary and ceremonial nature of the job.

In fact, accepting it had barred him from his real ambition of becoming prime minister. As Lord Chancellor he was merely the tip of the legal pyramid, yet this post was five centuries more ancient than that of prime minister and could be traced back to the seventh century. A document of 1068 refers to one of the King's chaplains as 'Cancellarius', who had custody of the royal seal by which royal letters were authenticated.

Baldwin refused to give Birkenhead the woolsack again because he was so often drunk. As a barrister he had quipped that he always drank two pints of beer at lunch 'to bring myself down to the level of the bench'. Instead he was made Secretary of State for India 'where he could do little harm and less work'. His retirement from politics in 1928 was received 'more with relief than regret'. As Laski put it: 'He has shot across politics like a meteor, and his disappearance leaves the sky unchanged.'

This was a pity because, a master of the stinging retort and venomous vituperation, he had a lightening wit and spell-binding oratorical gifts. He excelled at rugby, riding, golf and tennis and squandered several fortunes on brandy, boats, cards and cars, horses and houses. Winston Churchill observed that 'he burnt all his candles at both ends'. In 1928 his creditors forced him to resign from the government and he wrote several appallingly bad books to cover his debts. Nevertheless there was a sort of romance about him, a rags to riches shameless devotion to self advancement which 'gave ambition a bad name'.

Until he became Earl of Birkenhead, F.E. Smith always felt that his name lacked distinction. On one occasion he spelt Lady Wimborne's name wrongly. She said to him: 'How would you like it, Mr. Smith, if I misspelt your name?'

'My dear Lady, there is scarcely any alteration you could make which would not add to its distinction.'

F.E. Smith was notorious for his impertinence to hostile judges. His most famous exchange took place when he represented a tramway company which was being sued by a youth run over by a tram. Counsel for the boy asserted that he might suffer blindness as a result of the accident.

Judge Willis kept saying 'Poor boy, poor boy! Blind! Put him on a chair so that the jury can see him.'

Smith became impatient at this show of tearful prejudice. 'Perhaps your honour would like to have the boy passed round the jury-box?' he growled.

'You are extremely offensive, young man,' said the judge.

'As a matter of fact, we both are,' was the reply. 'The only difference is that I am trying to be and you can't help it.'

A barrister attempts to cross-examine a deaf witness, by Edward
Tennyson Reed, *The Sketch*, 1893 (Mary Evans Picture Library).

Later, Judge Willis again rebuked Smith: 'What do you suppose I am on the Bench for, Mr. Smith?'

'It is not for me to attempt to fathom the inscrutable workings of Providence,' he retorted.

One manoeuvre of F.E. Smith's is often cited as a classic of legal strategy. He was representing a bus company sued by the parents of a boy whose left arm was allegedly so damaged that he could only raise it to shoulder level. The boy was a pathetic figure, apparently still suffering great pain, and the jury were obviously sympathetic.

Smith began his cross-examination very gently: 'Please lift your arm as best you can.'

The boy raised his arm painfully to shoulder height.

'Thank you,' purred Smith silkily. 'And now can you please show us how high you could lift it before the accident?'

Without hesitation, the boy shot his injured arm straight up into the air.

ADVOCACY

When you have no basis for an argument, abuse the plaintiff.
> Cicero (106-43 BC)

So may the outward shows be least themselves;
The world is still deceived with ornament.
In law, what plea so tainted and corrupt
But, being seasoned with a gracious voice,
Obscures the show of evil?
> William Shakespeare (1564-1616),
> *The Merchant of Venice*
> 3.2 (1596-7)

Wherever you would persuade or prevail, address yourself to the passions; it is by them that mankind is to be taken. I bid you strike at the passions … if you can once engage people's pride, love, pity, ambition (or whichever is their prevailing passion) on your side, you need not fear what their reason can do against you.

> Lord Chesterfield (1694-1773),
> letter to his son (1746)

To win at law you need:
1. A good cause
2. A good purse
3. A skilful attorney
4. Good evidence
5. Able counsel
6. An upright judge
7. An intelligent jury
8. Good luck

> 'Eight Points of the Law' (1750), attributed
> to George Augustus Selwyn

A noisy man is always in the right.

> William Cowper (1731-1800)

A Chancery Suit

Mr Leach made a speech,
    Angry, neat, and wrong;
Mr Hart, on the other part,
    Was right, dull, and long.

Mr Bell spoke very well,
    Though nobody knew about what;
Mr Trower talked for an hour,
    Sat down, fatigued and hot.

In Court

Mr Parker made that darker,
    Which was dark enough without;
Mr Cooke quoted his book,
    And the Chancellor said, *I doubt*.

> Sir George Rose (1782-1873), Master in Chancery,
> referring to a case argued before Lord Eldon

I see you pay your lawyers not according to the length but according to the quality of their speeches.

> Comment on the brevity of English advocates in court,
> attributed to Georges Clemenceau (1841-1929)

One junior rose – with eyeballs tense,
And swollen frontal veins;
To all his powers of eloquence
He gave the fullest reins.
His argument was novel – for
A verdict he relied
On blackening the junior
Upon the other side.

> W.S. Gilbert (1836-1911), 'Damon v.
> Pythias', *The Bab Ballads* (1871)

'Where shall I begin, please your Majesty?' asked the White Rabbit.

'Begin at the beginning,' the King said gravely, 'and go on till you come to the end: then stop.'

> Lewis Carroll (1832-98), *Alice's
> Adventures in Wonderland* (1865)

A prosecuting attorney's success depends very largely on his ferocity. American practice permits him an extravagance of attack that would land him in jail, and perhaps even in a lunatic asylum, in any other country, and the more passionately he indulges in it the more certain becomes his promotion to higher office, including the judiciary.

> H.L. Mencken (1880-1956), *Notes on Democracy* (1926)

[The prosecutor] may prosecute with earnestness and vigour – indeed he shall do so. But, while he may strike hard blows, he is not at liberty to strike foul ones. It is as much his duty to refrain from improper methods calculated to produce a wrongful conviction as it is to use every legitimate means to bring about a just one.

> George Sutherland in *Berger* v. *United States* (1935)

The best way to discourage counsel if you think they are talking nonsense is to remain silent.

> Lord Kilbrandon (1906-89), Lord of Appeal

A trial is still an ordeal by battle. For the broadsword there is the weight of evidence; for the battle-axe the force of logic; for the sharp spear, the blazing gleam of truth; for the rapier, the quick and flashing knife of wit.

> Lloyd Paul Stryker, recalled on his death, 21 June 1955

I don't see why we should not come out roundly and say that one of the functions of a lawyer is to lie for his client; and on rare occasions, as I think I have shown, I believe it is.

> Charles P. Curtis, 'The Ethics of Advocacy', *Stanford Law Review* (1951)

The qualities essential to the successful practice of the art of advocacy cannot be acquired like pieces of furniture. Carson became an advocate because of parental pressure; Rufus

Isaacs only after he had been hammered on the Stock Exchange; Marshall Hall originally intended to enter the Church and changed his mind solely because he wanted to have enough money to get married.

> Richard Du Cann QC (1929-94),
> *The Art of the Advocate* (1964)

The right to begin is a priceless and often squandered asset.

> Richard Du Cann QC (1929-94),
> *The Art of the Advocate* (1964)

Next to the confrontation between two highly trained, finely honed batteries of lawyers, jungle warfare is a stately minuet.

> Bill Veeck, *The Hustler's
> Handbook* (1935)

I get paid for seeing that my clients have every break the law allows. I have knowingly defended a number of guilty men. But the guilty never escape unscathed. My fees are sufficient punishment for anyone.

> F. Lee Bailey, quoted in *Los Angeles
> Times*, 9 January 1972

Courtrooms contain every symbol of authority that a set designer could imagine. Everyone stands up when you come in. You wear a costume identifying you as, if not quite divine, someone special.

> Judge Irving R. Kaufman (1910-92),
> *Time Magazine*, 5 May 1980

Sir, the new series of *Kavanagh QC* is so true to life that I fell fast asleep during the last ten minutes of counsel's speech to the jury.

> Judge Barrington Black, letter
> to *The Times*, 9 March 1999

A barrister 'roasts' a shady witness while his colleagues listen
appreciatively, by Edward Tennyson Reed, *The Sketch*, 1893
(Mary Evans Picture Library).

I have always said that advocacy is like a battle. You plan it as best you can in advance, but when the battle takes place, nobody can quite foresee which way the tide will flow.

> George Carman QC, BBC Radio 4, 8 June 1999

EVIDENCE

Res ipsa loquitur
(The facts speak for themselves)

> Legal presumption

I will confess what I know without constraint; if ye pinch me like a pasty, I can say no more.

> William Shakespeare (1564-1616),
> *All's Well That Ends Well* 4.3
> (1602-3)

I confess nothing, nor I deny nothing.

> William Shakespeare (1564-1616),
> *Much Ado About Nothing* 4.1
> (1598-1600)

Where is the evidence that doth accuse me?
What lawful quest have given their verdict up
Unto the frowning judge?

> William Shakespeare (1564-1616),
> *Richard III* 1.4
> (1592-3)

… if I shall be condemn'd
Upon surmises – all proofs sleeping else
But what your jealousies awake – I tell you
'Tis rigour, and not law.

> William Shakespeare (1564-1616),
> *The Winter's Tale* 3.2
> (1610-11)

Othello: Villain, be sure thou prove my love a whore;
  Be sure of it. Give me the ocular proof,
  Or by the worth of mine eternal soul,
  Thou hads't better have been born a dog
  Than answer my waked wrath!
Iago: Is't come to this?
Othello: Make me to see't; or, at the least, so prove it
  That the probation bear no hinge or loop
  To hang a doubt on – or woe upon thy life!
>   William Shakespeare (1564-1616), *Othello* 3.3 (1604-5)

I'll see their trial first. – Bring in their evidence. –
Thou robed man of justice, take thy place.
>   William Shakespeare (1564-1616), *King Lear* 3.6 (1605-6)

  No, never say nothin' without you're compelled tu,
  An' then don't say nothin' thet you can be held tu.
>   James Russell Lowell (1819-91),
>   *The Biglow Papers*, Series II (1867)

And I would sooner trust the smallest piece of paper for truth,
than the strongest and most retentive memory ever bestowed
on mortal man.
>   Joseph Henry Lumpkin (1799-1867), US jurist, in
>   *Miller and others* v. *Cotton and others* (1848)

If a man go into the London Docks sober without any means
of getting drunk, and comes out of one of the cellars very
drunk wherein are a million gallons of wine, I think that
would be reasonable evidence that he had stolen some of the
wine in that cellar, though you could not prove that any wine
was stolen, or any wine was missed.
>   Sir William Henry Maule (1788-1858)
>   in *Reg.* v. *Burton* (1854)

In Court

Our duty is to believe that for which we have sufficient evidence, and to suspend our judgement when we have not.

John Lubbock (1803-65)

A witness cannot give evidence of his age unless he can remember being born.

Sir John Blagden (1908-85)

Some circumstantial evidence is very strong, as when you find a trout in the milk.

Henry David Thoreau (1817-62),
Journal, 11 November 1854

Take nothing on its looks; take everything on evidence. There's no better rule.

Charles Dickens (1812-70),
Great Expectations (1860-1)

'Give your evidence,' said the King; 'and don't be nervous, or I'll have you executed on the spot.'

Lewis Carroll (1832-98), *Alice's Adventures in Wonderland* (1865)

How often have I said to you that when you have eliminated the impossible, whatever remains, *however improbable*, must be the truth?

Sir Arthur Conan Doyle (1859-1930),
The Sign of Four (1890)

Even the clearest and most perfect circumstantial evidence is likely to be at fault, after all, and ought therefore to be received with great caution. Take the case of any pencil, sharpened by any woman: if you have witnesses, you will find she did it with a knife; but if you take simply the aspect of the pencil, you will say she did it with her teeth.

Mark Twain (1835-1910), *Pudd'nhead Wilson's Calendar* (1894)

Confession is the queen of evidence.

> Andrei Yanuaryevich Vyshinsky (1883-1954),
> Soviet lawyer, notorious prosecutor during
> the great purge trials of the 1930s

It took man thousands of years to put words down on paper, and his lawyers still wish he wouldn't.

> Mignon McLaughlin, *Saturday Review*

The plea of not guilty is a formal plea, which is merely a challenge to the prosecution to prove its case … Since the prisoner is presumed innocent until proved guilty, and it is always for the prosecution to prove guilt, there is no impropriety in fighting to show that the prosecution evidence has fallen short of proof; that is entirely different from being a party to putting before the court a positive defence known to be false.

> Sir Malcolm Hilbery (1883-1965),
> *Duty and Art in Advocacy* (1946)

The laws of evidence often prevent a person from telling the *whole truth*.

> Henry Cecil, *nom-de-plume* of
> Judge H.C. Leon (1902-76),
> *Hunt the Slipper*

The aims of cross-examination are two-fold: to weaken the case for the other side, and to establish facts which are favourable to the case for the cross-examiner.

> Richard Du Cann QC (1929-94),
> *The Art of the Advocate* (1964)

CROSS-EXAMINATION AND REPARTEE

More cross-examinations are suicidal than homicidal.
> Emory R. Buckner (1877-1941), in
> Francis L. Wellman, *The Art of*
> *Cross-Examination* (1936)

I never ask a question unless I know beforehand what the answer will be.
> Clarence S. Darrow (1857-1938), quoted in
> Irving Stone, *Clarence Darrow for*
> *the Defense* (1941)

The classic story about the extra question has to do with the man who was charged with mayhem. The allegation was that he was in a fight and the fight got rough and he bit the complainant's ear off. … So the case went to trial. A witness was on the stand and the defence lawyer took him over on cross-examination.

'Now, you saw this fight, did you?'

'Well, I didn't see all of it.'

'As a matter of fact, you didn't see very much of it, did you?'

'I didn't see very much of it, no.'

'As a matter of fact, you never saw the defendant bite the complainant's ear, did you?'

'No, I didn't.'

'But you testified that he bit it off, didn't you?'

'Yes.'

'Well, how did you know that the defendant bit the complainant's ear off?'

'Because I saw him spit it out.'
> Edward Bennett Williams (1920-88),
> 'You in Trial Law', in *Listen to*
> *Leaders in Law* (1963)

Judge Willis: Mr Smith, have you ever heard of a saying by Bacon – the great Bacon – that youth and discretion are ill-wed companions?

F.E. Smith: Indeed I have, Your Honour; and has Your Honour ever heard of a saying by Bacon – the great Bacon – that a much talking judge is like an ill-tuned cymbal?

> F.E. Smith (1872-1930), in *F.E.:*
> *The Life of F.E. Smith,*
> *by his son* (1959)

Master of the Rolls: Really, Mr Smith, do give this Court credit for some little intelligence.

F.E. Smith: That is the mistake I made in the Court below, m'lud.

> F.E. Smith (1872-1930)

Judge: I have read your case, Mr Smith, and I am no wiser now than when I started.

F.E. Smith: Probably not, my Lord, but far better informed.

> F.E. Smith (1872-1930), in *F.E.:*
> *The Life of F.E. Smith,*
> *by his son* (1959)

Counsel: You keep racehorses?
Horatio Bottomley: No.
Counsel: But you did keep racehorses?
Bottomley: No, never.
Counsel: You have a place in Sussex called The Dicker?
Bottomley: Yes.
Counsel: You have stables there – large stables?
Bottomley: Yes.
Counsel: You breed horses there – racehorses?
Bottomley: Yes.
Counsel: Then why did you tell me that you never kept racehorses?

Bottomley: I gave you a correct answer. I never kept racehorses. They keep me.

> Horatio William Bottomley (1860-1933),
> when questioned at his bankruptcy
> examination

Mr Barker, cannot you state your facts in some kind of order? Chronological is the best but, if you can't manage that, try *some* order. Why not alphabetical?

> Sir William Henry Maule
> (1788-1858)

Proceed. You have my biased attention.

> Judge Learned Hand (1872-1961),
> to attorney who asked to review
> a motion already heard

While engaged in cross-examining a witness at an Old Bailey trial William Rees-Davies (known at the Bar as 'Billy the One Armed Bandit', due to the loss of an arm during the war) kept receiving notes from the defendant as to the questions he should put. With each note the witness's replies became steadily more damaging to his client.

Finally Billy heaved a sigh as yet another note was passed to him by his instructing solicitor.

'Will your Lordship allow me a moment while I read the latest *billet doux* from my client?' he asked Judge Alan King-Hamilton.

'It may not be a *billet doux* this time,' retorted the Judge, 'it may be a Billy Don't.'

> Judge Alan King-Hamilton (1904-),
> recounted in 1999

JURY TRIAL

Ad quaestionem juris respondeant judices; ad quaestionem facti respondeant juratores.
(Let judges answer to the question of law, and jurors to the matter of fact.)

Legal maxim

A fox should not be of the jury at a goose's trial.
Proverb quoted by Thomas Fuller,
Gnomologia (1732)

> … I not deny
> The jury, passing on the prisoner's life,
> May in the sworn twelve have a thief or two
> Guiltier than him they try.

William Shakespeare (1564-1616),
Measure for Measure 2.1 (1604-5)

> Since twelve honest men have decided the cause,
> And were judges of fact, though not judges of laws.

William Pulteney, Earl of Bath
(1684-1764), 'The Honest Jury' in
The Craftsman (1731)

'Write that down,' the King said to the jury, and the jury eagerly wrote down all three dates on their slates, and then added them up, and reduced the answer to shillings and pence.
Lewis Carroll (1832-98),
*Alice's Adventures in
Wonderland* (1865)

> Now, Jurymen, hear my advice —
> All kinds of vulgar prejudice
> I pray you set aside:
> With stern judicial frame of mind

From bias free of every kind,
This trial must be tried.
>   W.S. Gilbert (1836-1911), *Trial by Jury* (1875)

We have a criminal jury system which is superior to any in the world and its efficiency is only marred by the difficulty of finding twelve men every day who don't know anything and can't read.
>   Mark Twain (1835-1910), speech on 'Americans
>   and the English', London, 4 July 1872

A jury too frequently have at least one member, more ready to hang the panel than to hang the traitor.
>   Abraham Lincoln (1809-65), letter to
>   Erastus Corning, 12 June 1863

[Members of the Bar] have been known to wrest from reluctant juries triumphant verdicts of acquittal for their clients, even when these clients, as often happens, were clearly and unmistakably innocent.
>   Oscar Wilde (1854-1900), *The
>   Decay of Lying* (1891)

'My Lord,' said the foreman of an Irish jury when giving in his verdict, 'we find the man who stole the mare not guilty.'
>   From *The Pun Book* by T.B.
>   and T.C. (1906)

The jury has the power to bring in a verdict in the teeth of both law and facts.
>   Oliver Wendell Holmes, Jr (1841-1935),
>   in *Horning* v. *District of*
>   *Columbia* (1920)

Jury: A group of twelve men who, having lied to the judge about their hearing, health and business arrangements, have failed to fool him.

> H.L. Mencken (1880-1956)

I may say after long experience that I have never yet known a case in which anything I have said has had any effect on a jury one way or another, and therefore I have come to the conclusion that the shorter the time I take in saying it the better for everyone.

> Sir Patrick Hastings KC (1880-1952), in
> *Laski* v. *Newark Advertiser* (1945)

No one has ever yet been able to find a way of depriving a British jury of its privilege of returning a perverse verdict.

> Lord Chief Justice Goddard
> (1877-1971), in the
> *Observer*, 1955

A jury is composed of twelve men of average ignorance.

> Herbert Spencer (1820-1903)

A jury consists of twelve persons chosen to decide who has the better lawyer.

> Robert Frost (1874-1963), quoted in
> Kenneth Redden, *Modern Legal
> Glossary* (1983)

If juries through sympathy do occasionally acquit a defendant whom the judge, applying the law strictly, would have convicted, it may be that that is one of the things that juries are for.

> Lord Diplock (1907-85), in
> *R.* v. *Lemon* (1979)

In Court

Juries are like Almighty God … totally unpredictable.
> John Mortimer (1923-), *The Trials*
> *of Rumpole* (1979)

A trial without a jury is like an operation without an anaesthetic, or a luncheon without a glass of wine.
> John Mortimer (1923-), *Rumpole*
> *for the Defence* (1981)

What makes juries worthwhile is that they see things differently from the judges … trial by jury is the lamp that shows that freedom lives.
> Lord Devlin (1905-92), *Sunday*
> *Times*, 18 April 1982

It's how a jury should be selected that's the problem. It used to be said that juries were entirely composed of middle-aged, middle-class men. That was true, but they came to some very reliable decisions.
> Lord Denning (1899-1999), *Sunday*
> *Times*, 1 August 1982

*

The Barrister's Dream

He dreamed he stood in a shadowy court,
    Where the Snark, with a glass in its eye,
Dressed in gown, bands, and wig, was defending a pig
    On a charge of deserting its sty.

The Witnesses proved, without error or flaw,
    That the sty was deserted when found:
And the Judge kept explaining the state of the law
    In a soft undercurrent of sound.

In Court

The indictment had never been clearly expressed,
    And it seemed that the Snark had begun,
And had spoken three hours, before anyone guessed
    What the pig was supposed to have done.

The Jury had each formed a different view
    (Long before the indictment was read),
And they all spoke at once, so that none of them knew
    One word that the others had said.

'You must know — ' said the Judge: but the Snark
    exclaimed, 'Fudge!
    That statute is obsolete quite!
Let me tell you, my friends, the whole question depends
    On an ancient manorial right.

'In the matter of Treason the pig would appear
    To have aided, but scarcely abetted:
While the charge of Insolvency fails, it is clear,
    If you grant the plea "never indebted".

'The fact of Desertion I will not dispute:
    But its guilt, as I trust, is removed
(So far as relates to the costs of this suit)
    By the Alibi which has been proved.

'My poor client's fate now depends on your votes.'
    Here the speaker sat down in his place,
And directed the Judge to refer to his notes
    And briefly to sum up the case.

But the Judge said he'd never summed up before;
    So the Snark undertook it instead,
And summed it so well that it came to far more
    Than the Witnesses ever had said!

Barristers in court, by Edward Tennyson Reed, *Punch*, 1892
(Mary Evans Picture Library).

When the verdict was called for, the Jury declined
    As the word was so puzzling to spell;
But they ventured to hope that the Snark wouldn't mind
    Undertaking that duty as well.

So the Snark found the verdict, although, as it owned
    It was spent with the toils of the day:
When it said the word 'GUILTY!' the Jury all groaned,
    And some of them fainted away.

In Court

Then the Snark pronounced sentence, the Judge being quite
　　Too nervous to utter a word:
When it rose to its feet, there was silence like night,
　　And the fall of a pin might be heard.

'Transportation for life' was the sentence it gave,
　　'And *then* to be fined forty pound.'
The Jury all cheered, though the Judge said he feared
　　That the phrase was not legally sound.

But their wild exultation was suddenly checked
　　When the jailer informed them, with tears,
Such a sentence would not have the slightest effect,
　　As the pig had been dead for some years.

The Judge left the Court, looking deeply disgusted;
　　But the Snark, though a little aghast,
As the lawyer to whom the defence was entrusted,
　　Went bellowing on to the last.

　　　　　　　　Lewis Carroll (1832-98), *The Hunting*
　　　　　　　　　　　of the Snark: An Agony in
　　　　　　　　　　　　　Eight Fits (1876)

LIBEL

A lawyer reads up on the law of libel, by 'Phiz', *Punch*, 1842
(Mary Evans Picture Library).

Libel

People in power do not like to be mocked. Roman law made singing abusive chants a capital offence. In Germanic law insults were punished by cutting out the tongue and early English law had similar penalties under King Alfred.

David Hooper, an authority on English libel law, traces its origin to the statute *Scandalum Magnatum* (Slander of Magnates) 1275. Peter Carter-Ruck goes even further back – to the Mosaic code, Exodus 23.1: 'Thou shalt not raise a false report.'

In the sixteenth century the going rate for libel was loss of the right hand and for slander, rather less logically, loss of the ears. In 1789 the editor of *The Times* accused the Prince of Wales of being less than sincere in his protestations of joy at the King's recovery of his health and spent more than a year in gaol.

In 1879 the editor of *Town Talk* got eighteen months for hinting that the Prince of Wales was having an affair with Lillie Langtry.

Insults were often the cause of duels. Young bloods were prone to bouts of ill-temper, apparently because of intestinal worms. It was common for a man to be killed.

William I had introduced the judicial duel as a means of settling disputes, and Trial by Battle was not abolished until 1819. The Court of Star Chamber exercised jurisdiction over libel to offer legal redress as an alternative to duelling.

The Merry Wives of Windsor begins with Justice Shallow

complaining of Falstaff's 'disparagements' of him and threatening to 'make a Star-Chamber matter of it; if he were twenty Sir John Falstaffs, he shall not abuse Robert Shallow esquire'. He then demands that the Privy Council 'shall hear it; it is a riot'. Sir Hugh Evans points out that the Privy Council does not deal with riots.

Clearly Shakespeare has in mind the essence of criminal libel which is that it tends to provoke a breach of the peace. Shallow is too old to challenge Falstaff to a duel but explodes:

'Ha! o'my life, if I were young again the sword should end it.'

It is apparent that in Shakespeare's day the English were a pretty violent lot.

Shakespeare uses the 'pound of flesh' fable as a comment on the current prevalence of duelling. In *The Merchant of Venice*, Shylock (who has merely been insulted) is prepared to butcher his insulter in public with impunity under the law, which is exactly what a skilled swordsman could do by provoking a duel. Portia invokes the law to prevent him.

A burlesque of a duel is a central feature of Shakespeare's play *Twelfth Night*. Sir Toby frightens Viola who is disguised as a man by telling her that her adversary, Sir Andrew Aguecheek, is 'a devil in private brawl. Souls and bodies hath he divorced three.'

Viola protests: 'I am no fighter. I have heard of some kind of men that put quarrels purposely on others to taste their valour: belike this is a man of that quirk.'

An ambush and murder could be disguised as a duel. Hence seconds were called in as witnesses. Sir Andrew's muddled letter of challenge turns the ambush onto himself:

> I will waylay thee going home, where if it be
> Thy chance to kill me …Thou killest me
> Like a rogue and a villain.

His challenge also contains accusations of lying, an unforgivable insult, automatically provoking a duel.

Nonetheless, says his friend Fabian, 'the wording of the challenge does not transgress the law'. He is probably referring to the civil law of slander. In his book *Miscellany-at-Law*, R.E. Megarry explains that in Tudor and Stuart times civil actions for slander flourished to such an extent that the judges tried to discourage litigation. In 1599 the allegation 'he is full of pox' was not actionable because the French pox was not specified. It could mean cow pox or small pox which are not venereal.

In 1618 the words 'Thou art a thieving whore and a pocky whore ...' were not actionable for the same reason. Moreover thieving might not be an accusation of felony.

In 1639 to say of a lawyer, 'He hath as much law as a Monkey' was not actionable because he had as much and might have more besides! But in 1594 a similar argument was rejected and the words 'He is a paltry lawyer, and has as much law as a jack-an-ape' resulted in £20 damages.

The English have long loved to mock their betters. Portia confesses in *The Merchant of Venice*: 'I know it is a sin to be a mocker.' She then goes on to poke fun at the English nobleman who has come to woo her.

Even judges sometimes cannot resist a little mockery at times, but are astute enough to 'wrap it up' in ambiguity. David Hooper spotted 'this remarkable passage' in the judgement of Lord Justice Scott in a libel case in 1943 concerning the meaning of the slang word 'pansy' in a cartoon in *Lilliput* magazine:

I personally was not alive to the slang meaning of the word, nor, I think, was my brother Mackinnon, but my brother Goddard fortunately was quite alive to it, having had judicial experience as a result of which he had come to know about it.

Pansy is a common term of abuse for the effeminate, although oddly enough other flowers such as daisy and lily are much older in this connection. Lord Goddard was well known for his peculiarities and his fellow appeal judge could not resist this unique opportunity for a veiled dig at him.

A fundamental feature of our libel law is that the parties' fate is decided by a jury as it is in a criminal trial. The jury must also assess without any guidance from the judge the amount of damages. Why a jury should be allowed to assess the value of a person's reputation is one of the mysteries of our law. It explains why some awards are ridiculously high. Why should a passing insult to a TV celebrity be worth more than the loss of limb?

In a criminal trial your fate depends on whether the jury likes your barrister. Whether you win a libel action depends on whether the jury likes *you*. In the newspaper world there is a saying: Never let the plaintiff get into the witness box.

R.E. Megarry in his *Miscellany-at-Law* refers to an American case where a wrestler was likened to a 'gorilla' in an educational article in a newspaper. In the ensuing action in 1930 the wrestler so charmed the jury that the compensation awarded astonished even his own lawyer.

'Words of heat or vulgar abuse' do not amount to slander unless they imply a specific crime or immoral conduct. 'He a justice of peace! He is an ass, and a beetle-headed justice.' These words were held not slanderous because a man 'cannot help his want of ability, as he may his want of honesty'.

Similarly, to say a justice is 'a fool or blockhead or a coxcomb and he knows no more than a slickhill' was held not an offence but a breach of good manners. However, you may not call your lawyer a 'Daffa-down-dilly' because this implies that he takes money from both sides.

A libel may still be prosecuted at common law as a crime if it is obscene or seditious and likely to provoke a breach of the peace. Truth itself is no defence to a *criminal* charge of libel, unless it is shown that the publication was for the public benefit. Hence the saying, 'The greater the truth, the greater the libel'.

*

Libel today is generally regarded as a civil matter to be dealt with by way of compensation and not in the criminal courts. This belief was shattered when Sir James Goldsmith tried to have Richard Ingrams, then editor of *Private Eye*, imprisoned. Goldsmith so terrified a reputable London solicitor called Leslie Paisner with similar threats of criminal libel that his health was broken and he died shortly afterwards.

'If your stockbroker cheats you, don't go round telling people he is a swindler. It is much cheaper to punch his head.' Much the same advice was given by his mother, a simple washer-woman, to Derek Jameson, who had been lampooned in a BBC radio skit as a 'tit and bum' journalist. He went to a fashionable solicitor who had won many libel claims, but before the case came on, the barrister sent in a very late opinion warning him that it was a 'high risk case' and he should settle on the best terms he could negotiate. Jameson complains he never saw this opinion until five years after he had lost the case, though he went on to make a highly successful career in broadcasting.

Michael Meacher too complained that his solicitor had failed to tell him that £225 had been paid into court which he could have accepted with an apology and not risked the enormous legal costs he had to pay when he lost. He eventually sued his solicitors. As a result of the same case his opponents, the *Observer*, also complained about their own solicitors who, they said, had unnecessarily prolonged the case by 'failures in communication'. The deputy editor of the *Observer* ultimately blamed Meacher's solicitor as 'the architect of the whole action'. The dispute was over whether or not Meacher's father was a farm labourer, as he claimed, or an accountant (i.e. not 'working class').

Even people who win their libel actions can risk financial ruin. Charlotte Cornwell was awarded £10,000 in 1985 for an abusive television review saying that her 'bum was too big'. But she had to go through three libel trials and one Court of Appeal hearing to get it and had to pay £70,000 legal costs herself, which compelled her to sell her house.

The saddest victim of his own libel action was the literary genius Oscar Wilde. The Marquess of Queensberry was furious at Wilde's homosexual relationship with his son and left a card at Wilde's club describing Wilde as a sodomite (which the Marquess in the heat of the moment misspelt 'somdomite'). In the ensuing libel prosecution of the Marquess, Wilde was torn to pieces in cross-examination and was himself later tried for homosexual offences and sent to prison. He died in poverty and disgrace.

In 1704 Chief Justice Holt referred to the cautionary case of the fellow who brought an action against another for saying he was a highwayman. It appearing on the evidence that he was indeed a highwayman, he was arrested in court, taken to Newgate, convicted at the following sessions and duly hanged.

*

So why do people bring libel actions? Is it misplaced pride? Once again we may turn to Shakespeare for an answer:

Cassio: Reputation, reputation, I ha' lost my reputation! I ha' lost the immortal part, sir, of myself and what remains is bestial; my reputation, Iago, my reputation!

Iago: … reputation is an idle and most false imposition, oft got without merit, and lost without deserving.

Adam Raphael, in his highly readable *Grotesque Libels*, tells us what it is like to be on both ends of a libel action, and also what it is like to be a witness in someone else's libel action. He gave evidence against Jeffrey Archer under sub-poena. A fellow journalist, a friend of Archer's, accused him of breach of his professional duty to his 'source'. Raphael then found himself bogged down in his own libel claim to clear his reputation, a claim which he eventually won hands down.

It would be a pity to abolish the law of libel and replace it with a system of published retraction and apology. In libel cases one sees the whole sweep of social history in its fascinating muddle, heartache, hypocrisy, spitefulness, greed, pride and sometimes outright lying.

Just as the close of the nineteenth century witnessed the spectacular fall from grace and imprisonment of the gifted poet Oscar Wilde, so the end of the twentieth century was marked by the self-destruction of a poetry-loving minister of the crown. Jonathan Aitken could not resist quoting from *Othello* (3.3) when he lied in his reply to the *Guardian*'s enquiry about payment of his bill at the Ritz Hotel in Paris:

> … Trifles light as air
> Are to the jealous confirmations strong
> As proofs of holy writ.

Perhaps he forgot that these words were spoken by Iago, uncrowned Prince of Liars. He should have heeded Chaucer's admonition against perjury in *The Pardoner's Tale* (quoted here from the Penguin translation by Nevill Coghill):

Now let me speak a word or two of swearing
And perjury; the Bible is unsparing.
It's an abominable thing to curse
And swear, it says; but perjury is worse.
Almighty God has said, 'Swear not at all,'
Witness St Matthew, and you may recall
The words of Jeremiah, having care
To what he says of lying; 'Thou shalt swear
In truth, in judgement and in righteousness,'
But idle swearing is a sin, no less.
Behold and see the tables of the Law
Of God's Commandments, to be held in awe;
Look at the third where it is written plain,
'Thou shalt not take the name of God in vain.'
You see He has forbidden swearing first;
Not murder, no, nor other thing accurst
Comes before that, I say, in God's commands.
That is the order; he who understands
Knows that the third commandment is just that.
And in addition, let me tell you flat,
Vengeance on him and all his house shall fall
That swears outrageously, or swears at all.

Slander-mongers and those who listen to slander, if I had my way, would all be strung up, the talkers by the tongue, the listeners by the ears.

Plautus (254-184 BC)

Innuendo into which one must read more meaning than was intended to meet the ear.

Seneca the Younger (c. 4 BC - AD 65),
Letters 114.1

The dead, having no rights, can suffer no wrongs.

Axiom of libel law

Do not wonder if the common people speak more truly than those of higher rank; for they speak with more safety.

Francis Bacon (1561-1626)

That is no slander, sir, which is a truth.

William Shakespeare (1564-1616),
Romeo and Juliet
4.1 (1595-6)

For slander lives upon succession,
For ever hous'd where it once gets possession.

William Shakespeare (1564-1616),
The Comedy of Errors
3.1 (1592-3)

He that filches from me my good name,
Robs me of that, which not enriches him,
And makes me poor indeed.

William Shakespeare (1564-1616),
Othello 3.2 (1604)

The effect of an amusing witness, by Edward Tennyson Reed,
The Sketch, 1893 (Mary Evans Picture Library).

Calumnies are answered best with silence.
Ben Jonson (1572-1637), *Volpone* 2.2 (1606)

Lie lustily, some filth will stick.
Thomas Hall (1610-65), *Funebria Florea* (1660)

Our disputants put me in mind of the scuttlefish that, when he
is unable to extricate himself, blackens the water around him
until he becomes invisible.
Joseph Addison (1672-1719), in
Spectator, 5 September 1712

Very few attacks either of ridicule or invective make much noise but with the help of those they provoke.

> Samuel Johnson (1709-84)

Calumny differs from most other injuries in this dreadful circumstance: he who commits it can never repair it.

> Samuel Johnson (1709-84)

No character, however upright, is a match for constantly reiterated attacks, however false.

> Alexander Hamilton (1755-1804), George
> Washington's aide-de-camp, before
> his death in a duel

Who shall estimate the cost of a priceless reputation – that impress which gives this dross its currency, without which we stand despised, debased, depreciated ...

> Charles Phillips, barrister, in a libel case,
> 1830, quoted by Richard Du Cann in
> *The Art of the Advocate* (1964)

A man is not stung the less by a libel because it happens to be true.

> Lord Abinger (1769-1844), in
> *Fraser* v. *Berkeley* (1836)

What is slander? A verdict of guilty pronounced in the absence of the accused, with closed doors, without defence or appeal, by an interested and prejudiced judge.

> Joseph Roux (1834-86), *Meditations
> of a Parish Priest* (1886)

A privileged occasion is one on which the privileged person is entitled to do something, which no one who is not within the privilege is entitled to do on that occasion. A person in such a position may say or write about another person things which no other person in the kingdom can be allowed to say or write. But, in the case of a criticism upon a published work, every person is entitled to do and is forbidden to do exactly the same things, and therefore the occasion is not privileged.

> Lord Esher (1817-99), in *Merivale*
> v. *Carson* (1887)

It is perfectly monstrous the way people go about nowadays saying things against one, behind one's back, that are absolutely and entirely true.

> Oscar Wilde (1854-1900), *The Picture*
> *of Dorian Gray* (1891)

I will make a bargain with the Democrats. If they will stop telling lies about the Republicans we will stop telling the truth about them.

> Chauncey Depew (1834-1928),
> US Republican politician

Very few people have ever embarked on a libel action without bitterly regretting their adventure before the case comes to trial.

> Sir Patrick Hastings (1880-1952), quoted by
> Adam Raphael, *Grotesque Libels* (1993)

One of the more elaborate means of using the law of libel to stifle criticism was that employed by Horatio Bottomley who wanted to suppress a pamphlet by Clarence Henry Norman entitled *Horatio Bottomley Exposed*. Bottomley could not sue Norman because what was written was true. He hit upon the idea of suing a tame printer who would print a few copies of Norman's pamphlet and admit he had libelled Bottomley: anyone planning to distribute Norman's publication would then be aware of the fact it had been adjudged libellous. He therefore approached his friend Reuben Bigland to find a printer he could sue. Bigland obliged with an ex-convict called John Greaney who was paid £50 for producing six copies.

Bottomley then sued 'this reckless printer' who did not appear at the trial, although he was waiting outside the court to receive another £50 when Bottomley obtained his verdict for £500. It did Bottomley little good, as he was soon to fall out with Bigland who himself wrote a similar pamphlet, *The Downfall of Horatio Bottomley MP – His Latest Greatest Swindle*. This time Bottomley issued proceedings for criminal libel against Bigland, although he was to offer no evidence and was in the end himself successfully prosecuted for fraud and sentenced to seven years' penal servitude.

David Hooper (1949-), *Public Scandal, Odium and Contempt* (1984)

Spoken words divorced from their context and surroundings may appear to be a slander which when controlled by such context and such surroundings are nothing of the sort. Gesture, tone of voice, expression of countenance, all of which are absent in libel may materially affect the spoken words. One recalls the instance of the lady who in a West End drawing-room accused a noble lord of being a thief, but when one is told that she said with a smile: 'Lord X, you are a thief, you have stolen my heart,' one recognises that to call a person a thief is not necessarily actionable.

Lord Justice Sankey (1866-1948), later Lord Chancellor, in *Broome* v. *Agar* (1928)

[In 1932 Norman Birkett appeared in] a macabre case in which a spiritualist medium named Mrs Meurig Morris brought a libel action against the publishers of the *Daily Mail* for exposing her spiritualistic performances as fraudulent and dishonest. The case, which was tried before Mr Justice

McCardie and a special jury in the Royal Courts of Justice in April 1932, caused the greatest public interest. During the eleven days of the trial, when forty witnesses were examined, the proceedings got remarkably out of hand, so much so that the exasperated judge had to adjourn them twice when the medium went into a trance in open court.

> H. Montgomery Hyde (1907-89), *The Life of Lord Birkett of Ulverston* (1964), describing *Morris* v. *Associated Newspapers Ltd.* (1932); Mrs Morris lost the case

In December 1916 ... Prince Philip Youssoupoff, with the very best of motives, had killed Gregory Rasputin. In the early 1930s Metro-Goldwyn-Mayer produced a film called *Rasputin – the Mad Monk*. The fact that Youssoupoff had killed Rasputin was a matter of common knowledge. There was little difficulty in the moderately well-informed film-goer identifying the film's characters Prince Paul and Princess Natasha Chegodieff as the Youssoupoffs. Unfortunately, the film contained a sequence which suggested that Rasputin was doing more than just hearing Princess Chegodieff's confessions.

Princess Youssoupoff sued and was awarded by the standards of the day the enormous sum of £25,000. Such was the size of the award that MGM soon heard from an actual Prince and Princess Chegodieff. Not surprisingly, MGM did not want another court case and so they agreed to pay them an undisclosed amount of libel damages – although, of course, the whole basis of the Youssoupoffs' claim was that anyone seeing the film must have concluded that the Chegodieffs were in fact the Youssoupoffs.

> David Hooper (1949-), *Public Scandal, Odium and Contempt* (1984)

Photographs have led to trouble. A press photograph of a policeman on point duty wiping his brow was used some years later, without his knowledge or consent, as an illustration for an advertising campaign which ran 'Phew! I am going to get my feet into a Jeyes fluid foot-bath.' The innuendo as to the policeman's feet and bodily condition cost the advertisers £100 in damages, with costs.

> R.E. Megarry (1910-), *Miscellany-at-Law* (1955),
> referring to *Plumb* v. *Jeyes' Sanitary
> Compounds Co. Ltd.* (1937)

An illustrated advertisement in an evening paper for an amusement device known as the 'Yo-Yo' once set out, with some circumstantial detail, the sad fate of a Mr Blennerhassett, 'as worthy a citizen as any that ever ate lobster at Pimm's' and regarded in Throgmorton Street as a sound man. The advertisement, which was headed 'Beware of Yo-Yo', described his purchase of a Yo-Yo for each of his children, his determined attempts to acquire the dexterity needed for mastery of the toy, his decline, and ultimately, his removal to 'a quiet place in the country'. Unfortunately, though the scriptwriter had not known it, there was a stockbroker called Blennerhassett, the only one of his name, and as soon as the advertisement appeared he was exposed to the full blast of Stock Exchange ribaldry and humour; and this, not surprisingly, disrupted his business. The paper published an apology, but nevertheless Mr Blennerhassett sued the advertisers and the paper. However, Branson J. held that no reasonable person could have thought that such an imaginative advertisement referred to any living person, and refused to allow the case to go to the jury.

> R.E. Megarry (1910-), *Miscellany-at-Law*
> (1955), referring to *Blennerhassett* v.
> *Novelty Sales Ltd.* (1933)

It is not in my opinion a statement of fact that a newspaper is low: it is a comment. It may be a statement of fact to say that a man is fraudulent, for there is a legal sanction for fraud, but there is no legal sanction for publishing low newspapers.

Lord Oaksey (1880-1971), in Kemsley v. Foot (1952)

Why should a claim for a damaged leg survive one's death whereas a claim for a damaged name does not? After death the leg cannot be healed, but the reputation can. To say that a man's defamed reputation dies with him is to ignore the realities of life and the bleak legacy he leaves behind.

Judge H. Lee Sarokin in US court ruling that the
family of a deceased man may sue for libel
to clear his name, 13 January 1983

If any of the imputations (i) are both factual and defamatory or (ii) are comment but could be made by an honest person on the facts; or (iii) are comment which an honest person could make but malice has been proved against the BBC — what damages do you award the Plaintiff?

Confusing 'guidelines' for jurors agreed by
lawyers in Jameson v. BBC (1984)

In some respects the law of libel is slanted in favour of the unmeritorious plaintiff. The issue of any writ for libel is a source of worry and expense to most defendants. It is the plaintiff who has control over the proceedings. Even if he ultimately loses the case, it will be some time before the defendant recovers his legal costs. However strong the defendant's case is, the court is very unlikely to allow him to recoup more than three-quarters of the fees he has had to pay his own lawyer. It is, therefore, a brave defendant who refuses to make any retraction.

David Hooper (1949-), Public Scandal,
Odium and Contempt (1984)

Libel is such a profitable High Court casino because only the rich can play.

> David Leigh (1947-), *Observer*,
> 28 April 1985

If this is justice, I am a banana.

> Ian Hislop (1960-), Editor of *Private Eye*, on the
> award of £600,000 damages to Sonia Sutcliffe
> against the magazine, 25 May 1989

We trust her gravy train has finally hit the buffers.

> Thomas Gerald Crone (1952-), legal manager of the *News
> of the World*, 21 December 1990, when Sonia Sutcliffe,
> who had won £500,000 from other newspapers, was
> finally defeated by the *News of the World*

In an unfortunate phrase, I told him not to go overboard.

> Joe Haines (1928-), *Daily Mirror*, advising Robert
> Maxwell on a libel suit shortly before Maxwell's
> body was found in the sea

Putting it bluntly, there is a need to discourage that small minority of plaintiffs who wish to proceed to trial from purely financial motives, especially in circumstances where the defendant is conceived to be 'over a barrel'.

> Lord Justice Neill (1923-), libel
> law report, July 1991

There are powerful forces, not least in Parliament, which see huge awards for damages in the High Court as the only way of restraining a prurient and licentious press. Many MPs would be sorry to see the opportunity for an occasional but useful tax-free bonus to their incomes taken from their grasp.

> Adam Raphael (1938-),
> *Grotesque Libels* (1993)

Verdict: £5,000 in compensatory damages, £50,000 in exemplary damages ... together with costs estimated at a quarter of a million pounds meant that *Private Eye* was over £300,000 out of pocket. After the case Robert Maxwell said he would devote the damages to AIDS research; 'The money from one infected organ will go to help cure another.'

> Adam Raphael (1938-),
> *Grotesque Libels* (1993)

If your lawyers tell you that you have a very good case, you should settle immediately.

> Richard Ingrams (1937-), on
> *Maxwell* v. *Private Eye*

Robert Maxwell ... a liar, a cheat and a bully [who] did more than any other individual to pervert the British law of libel.

> Obituary in the *Independent*, November 1991

The whole nonsense ... should be swept away – from grovelling apologies which nobody takes seriously to jury awards of damages which are based on no principle whatsoever.

> David Pannick QC (1956-), quoted by Adam
> Raphael (1938-), *Grotesque Libels* (1993)

The astronomical costs explain why the vast majority of actions – over 95 per cent – are settled out of court. The risk of losing forces the warring parties into settlement. The pressure is all the greater because of a tactical option open to the defence of paying into court anything from a ha'penny upwards. This ploy is designed to put the plaintiff on an even dicier spin of the roulette wheel. He can choose to accept the amount offered, which will bring the action to an end with most of the costs being met by the defendants. But if the sum paid into court is inadequate the risks are vastly increased. Unless the jury awards the plaintiff more than the payment into court, he will be responsible for all the costs from the time the payment into court was made. ...

In the famous case a generation ago of Lieutenant Colonel John Elliot Brooks, who had a taste for smacking the bottoms of young girls, the *Sunday People* was burdened with the costs of the trial after the former Mayor of Kensington and Chelsea was awarded a ha'penny damages by the jury. If the newspaper had paid even a penny into court, it would have had not just a moral but also a financial victory.

> Adam Raphael (1938-),
> *Grotesque Libels* (1993)

Love your enemy. It will ruin his reputation.

> Archbishop Desmond Tutu (1931-)

The first lesson of libel is, if you don't like losing, don't play the game.

> Thomas Gerald Crone (1952-), legal manager of
> the *Sun*, quoted in *The Times*, 26 January 1994,
> on Gillian Taylforth's defeat by the *Sun* after
> which she left court by ambulance

If newspaper vans ran amok in London and crashed freely into innocent pedestrians, that would cost their proprietors less than a few defamatory paragraphs.

> William Rees-Mogg (1928-),
> *The Times*, 27 January 1994

It's the decimals! It's the decimals! It's her next door, isn't it? I'll sue her for definition of character.

> Note taken at scene of noise source, read out at
> Horseferry Road Magistrates Court by John
> Pierce, Noise Officer, 1996

After a 314-day trial held over 2½ years – the longest in English history, costing an estimated £10 million – Mr Justice Bell ruled in June 1997 that some of the allegations in 'What's Wrong with McDonald's' were not libellous, but that others were. He awarded £60,000 damages against a former postman and a former gardener for libelling the corporation.

> Frances Gibb, *The Times*, 1 April 1999,
> reporting a subsequent Court of Appeal
> verdict reducing damages

Our law deters those who may have something of value to add to the public debate on the standards adopted by companies such as McDonald's. That is especially so where there is a lack of equality of arms, with the plaintiff able to employ lawyers of its choice and the defendants unable to claim legal aid, however strong their case on its merits. The McLibel case has achieved what many lawyers thought impossible; to lower further the reputation of our law of defamation in the minds of all right-thinking people. Libel law assumes that life is lived in a gentleman's club in which damage to reputation is one of the most serious injuries that a person can suffer. In defamation law, the proper response to an insult is to challenge the culprit to fight a high-risk public duel that can be avoided only by a grovelling apology and a large tax-free sum of damages.

> David Pannick QC (1956-), 'Exposing the flaws in
> Britain's libel laws', *The Times*, April 1999

If newspapers were honest I suspect they would admit to drawing actions out in the hope that a plaintiff runs up large legal bills, loses heart and settles.

> Justin Walford (1958-), legal adviser to the *Daily Express*,
> quoted by Adam Raphael, *Grotesque Libels* (1993):
> actual source uncertain, attribution denied

Libel will always attract the chancers as well as those seeking genuine vindication. The chances of success remain pretty good. For every Aitken, there are a hundred Liberaces or Maxwells, who emerge smiling from the High Court with a spotless reputation and a large tax-free sum.

> David Price (1963-), *Defamation,*
> *Procedure and Practice* (1999)

The court heard that when 'cornered' by newspapers and Granada TV's *World in Action*, Mr Aitken had made his most brazen move of all, issuing libel writs with the declaration: 'If it falls to me to start a fight to cut out the cancer of bent and twisted journalism in our country with the simple sword of truth and the trusty shield of British fair play, so be it.'

> *Independent*, 8 June 1999, after Jonathan Aitken had
> been sentenced to eighteen months imprisonment
> for perjury and perverting the course of justice

Not since the days of Oscar Wilde has a public figure who told a lie in a libel case suffered so much public humiliation.

> Sir John Nutting QC, pleading for
> leniency for Jonathan Aitken

*

Gordon-Cumming v. *Green*
(1891)

Sir William Gordon-Cumming ... owned two estates in Scotland, Altyre and Gordonstoun, with some 40,000 acres as well as a town house in London. He was the fourth baronet, a close friend of the Prince of Wales, and a Lieutenant-Colonel in the Scots Guards, much-decorated as a result of his exploits against the Zulus and the Egyptians and in the Nile Campaigns. ...

In September 1890 he joined a house party given by the nouveau-riche shipowners Mr and Mrs Arthur Wilson at Doncaster. The Prince of Wales was the principal guest. Gordon-Cumming had not originally been invited, but he was included at the request of the Prince and was accompanied by a subaltern in his regiment, Berkeley Levett.

On the first night the Prince proposed a game of baccarat, then generally considered a somewhat doubtful occupation. Like most games of chance, it was thought fairer if the participants staked their money before rather than after the fall of the cards was known. This was not the way Gordon-Cumming appeared to be playing. He was reckoned to be cheating by increasing his bet when the cards produced a winning score and withdrawing his counters when he lost – a dastardly trick known by the suitably Gallic name of *la poussette*. This was apparently spotted by the son of the house, Stanley Wilson, who whispered to Lieutenant Berkeley Levett: 'My God, Berkeley, this is too hot.'

After considerable discussion, it was decided to put the matter to the test the following night by chalking a white line on the green baize over which the players had to push their stakes. This merely confirmed their suspicions about Gordon-Cumming, who had won £228, principally from the Prince of Wales. He was accused of cheating by two other members of the house party, General Owen Williams and the Earl of Coventry. Despite his protestations of innocence, Gordon-Cumming was persuaded to sign a solemn undertaking never to play cards again so long as he lived. This he did to avoid a scandal involving the Prince of Wales, in itself a somewhat uphill task. (As it was, Gordon-Cumming subpoenaed the Prince as a witness at the subsequent trial.)

Gordon-Cumming left the house party the next day, but his secret undertaking soon became the subject of considerable gossip. Eventually he received, two days after Christmas, an anonymous letter written from Paris signed by 'Someone who pities you' who clearly had heard most of the details of the scandal. Gordon-Cumming felt he had to sue and he issued proceedings for slander against Levett, Mr and Mrs Wilson and Mr and Mrs Lycett Green, his less blue-blooded accusers.

Much has been written of the proceedings before Lord Chief Justice, Lord Coleridge. Certainly the way the case was conducted left much to be desired. Admission to the court-room was by ticket signed by the Lord Chief Justice, who had appropriated half of them for his friends who came to court with their opera glasses. His family played an important role in the trial, his daughter sketching the scene and his wife periodically prodding the dozing septuagenarian judge.

The number of witnesses against Gordon-Cumming, the undertaking he had signed, the amount he had won and the evidence of his erstwhile friend the Prince of Wales made the result inevitable. ...

The jury took only thirteen minutes to find against Gordon-Cumming. The result was, however, greeted with jeers and there were those who believed in his innocence. Sir Edward Clarke QC, his counsel and the Solicitor General, was to write in his memoirs: 'I believe the verdict was wrong and Sir William Gordon-Cumming was innocent of the offence charged against him.' Gordon-Cumming's wife was convinced that the accusation was engineered by the Prince of Wales to settle a score with Gordon-Cumming over his affair with the Prince's mistress, Lady Frances Brooke.

The evidence against Gordon-Cumming was however extremely strong. (He was a man who once boasted that he had broken every commandment except that against murder.) In any event his ruin was swift and complete. He had to resign from the army, leave Court, and he was expelled from the Carlton, Turf, Marlborough and Guards Clubs. He did not again grace London or the racecourse, the hunting field or any of the fashionable resorts of the era. For the remaining forty years of his life he lived outside society at Altyre, dying in 1930, still protesting his innocence. The seal had been put upon his ruin by his libel action.

David Hooper (1949-), *Public Scandal,*
Odium and Contempt (1984)

Mountbatten v. *Odhams Newspapers* (1932)

Edwina Mountbatten had become friendly with the black American actor, Paul Robeson, following his success in London in the role of Othello. Robeson was frequently to be seen at the Mountbattens' parties at Brook House. It was at that time most unusual to see a black person in fashionable society and his friendship with Edwina became well known.

However, it was one thing for this association to be discussed in polite society. It was apparently quite another for it to be commented on in the popular press. In May 1932 *The People* published an article in its gossip column:

FAMOUS HOSTESS EXILED
SOCIETY SHAKEN BY
TERRIBLE SCANDAL

I am able to reveal today the sequel to a scandal which has shaken Society to the very depths. It concerns one of the leading hostesses in the country, a woman highly connected and immensely rich.

Associations with a coloured man became so marked that they were the talk of the West End. Then one day the couple were caught in compromising circumstances.

The sequel is that the Society woman has been given the hint to clear out of England for a couple of years to

let the affair blow over, and the hint comes from a
quarter that cannot be ignored.

The quarter which could not be ignored was a none too
oblique reference to Buckingham Palace. Edwina was compelled to sue to deny that she had an association with a
coloured man and that she had been ordered to live abroad.

David Hooper (1949-), *Public Scandal,
Odium and Contempt* (1986 edition)

'It is not too much to say that it is the most monstrous and
most atrocious libel of which I myself in all my experience in
these courts have ever heard,' said Birkett in opening the case
before the Lord Chief Justice, Lord Hewart. 'Your lordship
may think that the word "scandal" at the top of the article
coupled with the words, "the hint comes from a quarter that
cannot be ignored", puts it beyond all doubt that the writer
deliberately intended to defame Lady Louis Mountbatten. It
is unnecessary to say that there is not one word of truth in
these horrible allegations. Nor is there the faintest ground
upon which these lying rumours could be brought into existence at all.' Birkett went on to say that the defendants were
willing to pay damages, and there was not the smallest doubt
that a jury would have awarded very heavy damages, but
Lady Louis refused to accept one single penny which would
to her be 'in the highest degree distasteful'. What she did
desire was that there should be a speedy and public vindication of her name in the fullest possible manner, and with this
end in view her counsel asked that 'in the very exceptional
circumstances of this case', she and her husband might be
allowed to go into the witness box. Lord Hewart agreed.

Lord Louis Mountbatten was the first to give evidence. He
told the court how, as a naval officer attached to the Mediter-
ranean Fleet, he had been ordered to Malta for two years and

it was natural that his wife and children should follow him there for the duration of his appointment. Lady Louis then entered the witness box. Replying to her counsel's questions, she declared that she had returned to this country from Malta solely in order to give evidence in this case.

Birkett held up a copy of the offending journal. 'The second paragraph in this publication deals with a coloured man,' he said. 'Is there one single word of truth in the allegation there made?'

'Not one single word,' Lady Mountbatten replied in ringing tones. 'In fact, I have never in the whole course of my life met the man referred to.'

'Your friends have named to you the coloured man supposed to be referred to in the paragraph?' continued Birkett.

'They have,' admitted Lady Mountbatten.

'And you have never had anything to do with him in any shape or form?'

'The whole thing is a preposterous story.'

'Was it your desire, when the article was brought to your notice, that you should have the opportunity of going into the witness box to deny this horrible thing on oath?'

'It was my express wish.'

For the defendants, Sir Patrick Hastings made an unqualified apology, coupled with 'genuine and deep regrets', and reiterated the newspaper's willingness to pay damages, which Hastings agreed if awarded by a jury must have been extremely heavy. It was also intimated that the person responsible for the gossip column had been dismissed as soon as the proprietors of *The People* had received Lady Louis Mountbatten's complaint.

'One does not wonder that in these circumstances the plaintiff does not desire damages,' Lord Hewart observed. 'I should have been astonished if she had accepted them because there are some libels which are crimes on the part of every-body concerned.'

In agreeing to Birkett's request that the record should be withdrawn on the terms that the defendants apologised and paid all the plaintiff's costs and expenses, the Lord Chief Justice made it clear that he did so 'with considerable doubt and hesitation' in view of the possibility of criminal proceedings being instituted. As it was, Lord Hewart ordered that a copy of the paper should be kept in the custody of the court, and the editor was fortunate in escaping prosecution for criminal libel.

H. Montgomery Hyde (1907-89), *The Life of Lord Birkett of Ulverston* (1964)

Beloff v. *Private Eye* (1972)

Auberon Waugh wrote a satirical piece in his political column, HP Sauce [in *Private Eye*], about 'the delicious 78-years-old Nora Ballsoff' adding, 'Miss Bailiff, sister of the late Sir Alec Douglas Home, was frequently to be seen in bed with Mr Harold Wilson and senior members of the previous administration, though it is thought nothing improper happened.'

This edition of *Private Eye* resulted in two writs … In the event, Nora Beloff lost the copyright case [*Private Eye* had published one of her internal memoranda without permission] on a technicality, the judge holding that the copyright of her memorandum belonged to the *Observer*. On the libel she fared better, being awarded £3,000 damages and £2,000 costs.

The result, though, was a Pyrrhic victory for the *Observer*'s Political Correspondent. …*Private Eye* decided to exact cruel revenge. This consisted of setting up a fund to pay its libel costs – 'the Ballsoff fund' – which was publicised month after month alongside a grim-faced photograph of the victim. It raised more than £1,200 from contributors.

Adam Raphael (1938-),
Grotesque Libels (1993)

If Miss Beloff's copyright action had succeeded, it would have rendered almost impossible some of the most important and valuable contributions the press makes to public life ... As for her libel action, it has made even the wildest fantasies and jokes dangerous, if they are to be made about somebody with a seemingly underdeveloped sense of humour.

Bernard Levin (1928-), *The Times*,
October 1972

Lampooning the establishment is age-old. It has been done in all civilised societies and it is the hallmark of a civilised society that there should be a good deal of satirical writing and taking the wind out of unnecessarily puffed sails. ... But it has always been the law that one who defamed a person as a jest did so at his peril.

Mr Justice O'Connor (1914-),
summing up to the jury

Goldsmith v. *Private Eye* (1977)

What happens when you cross a bitterly angry, obsessive multi-millionaire was now to be revealed. An avalanche of 90 separate writs for libel descended on *Private Eye* and its wholesale and retail distributors. The next eighteen months witnessed one of the most spectacular and expensive battles in British legal history, involving ten court hearings and the expenditure of at least £500,000. Goldsmith was on solid ground in that he had clearly been defamed. If he had proceeded in the normal way he could confidently have expected to receive six-figure damages.

Calculating, however, that *Private Eye* merely thrived on the publicity generated by libel actions, Goldsmith made the mistake of overreacting, spraying writs in all directions and seeking to jail the writers of the offending article by means of a criminal indictment. When Goldsmith was asked at the criminal libel proceedings about the large number of writs he had issued against *Private Eye*, he replied that he had previously issued only one against a newspaper. 'You are making up for it now,' commented the *Eye*'s counsel, James Comyn QC. By reviving the archaic proceeding of the criminal prosecution for libel with its threat of imprisonment against Ingrams (editor of *Private Eye*) and his colleagues, Goldsmith appeared vindictive. And by proceeding against many of the *Eye*'s smaller distributors, he seemed to be an enemy of the freedom of the press.

What Goldsmith did not appreciate was that libel actions are essentially a battle for public opinion. And the methods of a tycoon are not those best suited to win such a contest. At one point he employed 'a highly reputable' firm of private detectives to go through *Private Eye*'s dustbins each night. They took out the contents, photocopied them, and then replaced them – so that they could not be charged with theft. Lunches of *Eye* journalists were electronically bugged by placing a minute listening device on a coat-stand. ... In May 1977 he agreed to call off his criminal libel action on condition that *Private Eye* published a full-page apology in the *Evening Standard*.

... But, money apart, the case was a disaster for him. The widespread hostility it aroused destroyed any hopes he might have had of either a political career or of becoming a British newspaper baron.

Adam Raphael (1938–),
Grotesque Libels (1993)

CRIME AND PUNISHMENT

Mr Baron Martin dons the black cap to pass the death sentence on
Muller, the railway murderer, *The Illustrated Times*, 1864
(Mary Evans Picture Library).

Crime and Punishment

A broad definition of crime in England is that it is any lower-class activity which is displeasing to the upper class. Crime is committed by the lower class and punished by the upper class.

David Frost and Anthony Jay,
To England with Love (1967)

In 1918 a mob attacked Bertrand Russell while he was delivering an anti-war speech. A friend rushed over to some police officers and pleaded with them to protect Russell, but they merely shrugged.

'But he is world famous!' exclaimed the friend.

The police made to leave the scene of the disturbance.

'He is the brother of an earl!' cried the friend desperately.

The policemen hurried back with truncheons drawn to rescue Russell.

*

Anyone proposing to embark on a life of crime, a leading barrister once remarked, would be safest devising some form of fraud. Even when caught, the white-collar fraudster is seldom severely punished and may well serve any sentence in an open prison.

The chances of a fraudster escaping the jaws of justice are more favourable than for any other type of crime. Many years ago a cashier gambled away some £20,000 of his firm's money. He knew that the deficiency would shortly be discovered on audit, so he took what little cash he could muster to the President of the Law Society and asked his advice.

'Do you think you could manage to siphon off another £10,000 without being discovered?' asked the President.

'Certainly.'

'Then do so and bring it to me as soon as possible.'

As soon as the money was on his desk, the President telephoned the firm's Managing Director and told him that one of his employees had embezzled £30,000 but that he was in a position to refund £10,000 on the understanding that there was no prosecution. The Managing Director consulted his Board at an emergency meeting, and they decided that a bird in the hand was worth two in the bush. The cashier duly escaped his just deserts.

*

Ignorance of the law excuses no man; not that all men know the law, but because 'tis an excuse every man will plead, and no man can tell how to confute him.

John Selden, jurist and
antiquary (1584-1654)

Ignorantia legis neminem excusat (ignorance of the law excuses no man from obeying it), is a saying almost as old as the law itself.

Unwitting violation of traffic regulations is an example of the smart we all feel at the law's unfairness. But no other rule would be workable. Otherwise we could all commit the most heinous crimes with impunity, provided we took care to keep ourselves ignorant of what the law is. It would be impossible to convict those who stoutly maintained their ignorance.

A man who had been at sea when a law was passed returned home to find himself prosecuted for something that was not made illegal until after he left. This was a rare case when such a defence was allowed to succeed.

*

Not everyone is in favour of the abolition of capital punishment. A Lord of Appeal is alleged to have commented *sotto voce* of the appeal of the Birmingham Six: 'If we'd retained hanging, we wouldn't have had all this trouble.'

On the other hand, Albert Pierrepoint, the chief public hangman from 1946 to 1956, declared in his autobiography: 'Capital punishment, in my view, achieved nothing but revenge.' During his career he disposed of 433 men and seventeen women, including Ruth Ellis, the last woman to be executed in Britain. He followed in the family profession and as a twelve-year-old schoolboy had contemplated his career with relish in a school essay: 'I would like to be a public executioner as my dad is because it needs a steady man with good hands like my dad and uncle Tom and I shall be the same.'

Another devotee of hanging who later changed his mind was Leslie Boyd, the Clerk of the Court at the Old Bailey for 36 years until he retired in 1977. He at first regretted the abolition of capital punishment on the ground that 'All the atmosphere and steam had been taken out of murder trials', but with the passage of time he came to realise that its abolition had released the judicial process from enormous strain. When its reintroduction was mooted he remarked, 'We can't go back to that.'

In 1885 John Lee, condemned to death by hanging at Exeter prison, was reprieved when the trap door failed to open after the third try. Earlier in the century in the USA a man escaped hanging because on the first attempt the rope broke, on the second attempt the new rope stretched and let his feet touch the ground, and finally a third rope broke. In accordance with tradition he too was reprieved.

*

In 1999 the prison population of the UK was above 65,000. In all about 110,000 prisoners go through our 135 jails annually. Keeping people in prison or even in a police cell overnight is more expensive than putting them up at a first-class hotel in central London. But it is not necessary to have a prison population of the size of a major town. In reality only violent or habitual criminals need to be locked up. The rest could be let out on bail, particularly those who are awaiting trial. The problem is, where would they go? In a society which refuses to have a system of identification (which almost all other European countries employ) it is easy to vanish into the general population. This makes it very difficult and expensive to track down absconders until they are caught re-offending. The ingrained British opposition to identity cards is likely to last until crime becomes a threat even to the most privileged.

Profile of a Rogue

Horatio Bottomley (1860-1933)
Journalist, politician, financier and bankrupt

Horatio William Bottomley proved himself a match for many of the outstanding lawyers of his day. He was a journalist who got his legal training the hard way by defending himself in a series of libel cases while at the same time employing a barrister, often Sir Edward Marshall Hall, to defend his newspaper. Marshall Hall once told Bottomley that he could have made a brilliant career for himself at the bar. Mr Justice Hawkins described him as the ablest advocate he had ever heard, and offered to lend him his wig.

As a journalist Bottomley was eminently successful. In 1888 he founded the *Financial Times*, in 1906 *John Bull*, and in the same year he was elected to parliament as a Liberal MP. At heart, however, he was a rogue. His newspaper empire collapsed in 1888 with a capital loss of £1 million (then a colossal sum). He was prosecuted but secured his acquittal himself by his skilful defence.

During the First World War he made stirring speeches for the recruitment drive. But after the war his Victory Bond Club got him into trouble with the law again, and this time he was sent to prison for seven years. Even this spell behind bars could not destroy his ebullient jocularity. A few days after his release he was seen lunching in Romano's by Sir Henry Curtis Bennett who remarked how well he was looking. Bottomley surveyed Sir Henry's ample paunch: 'It looks as if three years would not do you much harm either.'

Bottomley was an immensely resourceful opponent. A court order was once made against him obliging him to produce certain account books. Their disclosure would have demolished his case and probably have landed him in prison.

On the arrival of the bailiff who had come to collect them, Bottomley said that they were much too bulky to carry. He accordingly sent for a taxi and the books were duly loaded onto the back seat. Just as the taxi was about to depart Bottomley called to the bailiff from his flat and asked for a written receipt.

The bailiff went up, wrote out a receipt and left the building, only to find that the taxi had vanished. The incriminating books were never seen again.

During one of his numerous libel actions Bottomley was heard to remark to a friend on leaving court with a verdict in his favour: 'What a nice old gentleman the judge is! He let me say what I liked. I think I shall retain him to hear all my future cases.'

He once made a fool of no less an advocate than Sir John Simon, who had called a certain Mr Murray to testify against Bottomley. Murray was not being very helpful to Sir John's case:

'So Mr Bottomley invited you to luncheon, Mr Murray. Please tell the jury what took place.'

'Well, I arrived at the restaurant.'

'Yes, what then?'

'I went and washed my hands.'

'Yes, yes, but what happened at the actual luncheon?'

'First of all, we had some hare soup and dumplings. Yes, I'm sure there were dumplings. Then we had fried smelts; and then – yes, to be sure – Mr Bottomley ordered two portions of roast saddle of mutton.'

'Sir John Simon began to lose his cool. 'Yes, yes, Mr Murray, but please …'

At this juncture Bottomley jumped to his feet and protested to the judge:

'I really must ask your lordship to stop learned counsel interrupting his own witness. What about the vegetables? Mr Murray wants to tell us about the *vegetables*.'

However, Bottomley was worsted by the great F.E. Smith, whom he congratulated on his appointment as Lord Chancellor. Incautiously Bottomley added the jibe:

'Upon my soul, F.E., I shouldn't have been surprised to hear that you had been made Archbishop of Canterbury.'

'If I had,' replied the Lord Chancellor, 'I should have asked you to my installation.'

'That's damn nice of you,' said Bottomley.

'Not at all. I should have needed a crook.'

While serving a prison sentence for misappropriation of

vast funds, he was spotted sewing mail bags by a prison visitor who knew him personally. 'Ah, Bottomley, I see you are busy sewing,' he remarked.

Bottomley showed no rancour or embarrassment.

'No, simply reaping,' he replied.

He was brought from prison one day for examination at the Bankruptcy Court. He appeared dressed in his own suit which was noticeably creased through storage at the prison. A friend met him by chance in court and commented on the state of his coat.

'Never mind! When I get back, I change for dinner,' replied Bottomley.

In any case of injustice it makes a great difference whether the wrong is done on impulse, or whether it is committed deliberately and with premeditation; for offences committed on impulse are less culpable than those committed by design and with malice.

Cicero (106-43 BC), *De officiis* 1.7

Nemo repente fuit turpissimus.
(No one ever suddenly became depraved.)
Juvenal (AD *c.* 60 – *c.* 130), *Satires*

Whoever secretly meditates a crime is as guilty as he who carries it out.

Juvenal (AD *c.* 60 – *c.* 130), *Satires*

The sin is in itself excusable; to be taken is a crime.
John Fletcher (1579-1625),
Lover's Progress 4.1 (1623)

If poverty is the mother of crime, stupidity is its father.
La Bruyère (1645-96), 'Of Man'
in *Characters* (1688)

We must conceal crimes we cannot cure.
Daniel Defoe (1660-1731), *The True-born
Englishman* (1701)

But if he does really think that there is no distinction between virtue and vice, why, Sir, when he leaves our houses, let us count our spoons.

Samuel Johnson (1709-84), of James Macpherson,
14 July 1763, quoted by James Boswell, *Life of
Samuel Johnson* (1791)

Crime and Punishment

If once a man indulges himself in murder, very soon he comes
to think little of robbing; and from robbing he comes next to
drinking and sabbath-breaking, and from that to incivility and
procrastination. Once begun upon this downward path, you
never know where you are to stop.

Thomas De Quincey (1785-1859), 'On Murder
Considered as One of the Fine Arts',
Blackwood's Magazine, November 1839

C'est pire qu'un crime, c'est une faute.
(It's worse than a crime, it's a blunder.)

Antoine Boulay de la Meurthe (1761-1840),
on hearing of the execution of the Duc
d'Enghien by Napoleon

I met a cracksman coming down the Strand,
  Who said, 'A huge Cathedral, piled of stone,
 Stands in a churchyard, near St Martin's Le Grand.
  Where keeps St Paul his sacerdotal throne.
A street runs by it to the northward. There
For cab and bus is writ, "No Thoroughfare",
  The Mayor and Councilmen do so command,
And in that street a shop, with many a box,
  Upon whose sign these fateful words I scanned:
"My name is Chubb, who makes the Patent Locks;
  Look on my works, ye burglars, and despair!"'
Here made he pause, like one who sees a blight
  Mar all his hopes, and sighed with drooping air,
'Our game is up, my covies, blow me tight!'

Sir Theodore Martin (1816-1909), parody
of Shelley's 'Ozymandias', from
The Thieves' Anthology

In 1811 Mr Purcell of Co. Cork, a septuagenarian, was knighted for killing four burglars with a carving knife.

> Footnote to *Kenny's Outlines of Criminal Law* (1952), in another version reduced to two burglars

When the righteous man turneth away from his righteousness that he hath committed and doeth that which is neither quite lawful nor quite right, he will generally be found to have gained in amiability what he has lost in holiness.

> Samuel Butler (1835-1902),
> *Notebooks* (1912)

A Wanted Absconder

About 48 years of age, in height about 5 ft 6 in to 5 ft 7 in, stout build, sharp abrupt manner, large bald head, short nose, sometimes wearing a wig, has a flat face and prominent chin, and having lost many teeth, the nose and chin appear to be sometimes drawn towards each other, one of the fingers on the right hand has been cut or otherwise injured at the end, a swaggering gait and rather large whiskers and generally well dressed for a man of his station of life.

> *The Times*, 1835

A clever theft was praiseworthy amongst the Spartans; and it is equally so amongst Christians, provided it be on a sufficiently large scale.

> Herbert Spencer (1820-1903),
> *Social Statics* (1851)

The Latest Decalogue

Thou shalt have one God only; who
Would be at the expense of two?
No graven images may be
Worshipped, except the currency:
Swear not at all; for, for thy curse
Thine enemy is none the worse:
At church on Sunday to attend
Will serve to keep the world thy friend:
Honour thy parents; that is, all
From whom advancement may befall;
Thou shalt not kill; but needs't not strive
Officiously to keep alive.
Do not adultery commit;
Advantage rarely comes of it:
Thou shalt not steal; an empty feat,
When it's so lucrative to cheat;
Bear not false witness; let the lie
Have time on its own wings to fly:
Thou shalt not covet, but tradition
Approves all forms of competition.

Arthur Hugh Clough (1819-61),
Poems (1862)

Ex-Professor Moriarty of mathematical celebrity ... is the Napoleon of Crime, Watson.

Sir Arthur Conan Doyle (1859-1930),
'The Final Problem' in *The Memoirs of Sherlock Holmes* (1894)

Smiling Villain

Forth from his den to steal he stole,
His bags of chink he chunk,
And many a wicked smile he smole,
And many a wink he wunk.

Anon.

The Village Burglar

Under a spreading gooseberry bush the village burglar lies.
The burglar is a hairy man with whiskers round his eyes,
And the muscles of his brawny arms keep off the little flies.

He goes on Sunday to the church to hear the parson shout.
He puts a penny in the plate and takes a sovereign out,
And drops a conscience-stricken tear in case he is found out.

Anon.

Thieves respect property; they merely wish the property to
become their property that they may more perfectly respect it.

G.K. Chesterton (1874-1936),
The Man Who Was Thursday
(1908)

Late last night I slew my wife,
Stretched her on the parquet flooring.
I was loth to take her life,
But I *had* to stop her snoring!

Harry Graham (1874-1936),
*Ruthless Rhymes for Heartless
Homes* (1899)

There was an old fellow of Lympne
Who married three wives at one time;
    When asked: 'Why the third?'
    He replied, 'One's absurd;
And bigamy, Sir, is a crime.'

                                  Anon.

No matter how hard the times get, the wages of sin are always liberal and on the dot.

                          Kin Hubbard (1868-1930)

Everybody is a potential murderer. I've never killed anyone, but I frequently get satisfaction reading the obituary notices.

                     Clarence S. Darrow (1857-1938),
                     New York Times Magazine,
                            18 April 1937

There are only about twenty murders a year in London and not all are serious—some are just husbands killing their wives.

                     Commander G.H. Hatherill of Scotland
                     Yard, *Observer* Sayings of the Week,
                          21 February 1954

How many crimes are committed merely because their perpetrators could not endure being wrong!

                   Albert Camus (1913-60), *La Chute* (1956)

Crime is a logical extension of the sort of behaviour that is often considered perfectly respectable in legitimate business.

                     Robert Rice (1916-), *The Business
                           of Crime* (1956)

It ain't no sin if you crack a few laws now and then, just so long as you don't break any.

                   Attributed to Mae West (1892-1980)

Mass murderers are simply people who have had *enough*.
Quentin Crisp (1908-), *The Naked
Civil Servant* (1968)

I think crime pays. The hours are good. You travel a lot.
Woody Allen (1935-), *Take the
Money and Run* (1969)

The American dream is, in part, responsible for a great deal
of crime and violence because people feel that the country
owes them not only a living but a good living.
Davin Abrahansen, psychoanalyst, in *San
Francisco Chronicle*, 18 November 1975

Nothing is illegal if 100 businessmen decide to do it.
Andrew Young (1932-),
US politician (1976)

Being a thief is a terrific life, but the trouble is they put you
in the nick for it.

John McVicar, reformed
criminal, *Observer*

I know it when I see it.

Mr Justice Stewart, US Supreme
Court (1964), when asked for a
definition of obscenity

The test of obscenity under the Obscene Publications Act
1959 is whether material is such 'as to tend to deprave and
corrupt persons who are likely to read see or hear the matter'.
The test is *not* whether such material is repulsive, filthy,
loathsome or lewd.
Lord Chief Justice Widgery in
the *Oz* case, Court of
Appeal (1971)

At the showing of blue movies at Scotland Yard I take the precaution of removing my glasses, which reduces the whole messy business to an impressionist blur.

> John Mortimer QC (1923-), *Clinging to the Wreckage* (1982)

Parliament itself would not exist in its present form had people not defied the law.

> Arthur Scargill (1938-) to House of Commons Select Committee on Employment, 2 April 1980

A kleptomaniac is a person who helps himself because he can't help himself.

> Anon.

Murder is a crime. Describing murder is not. Sex is not a crime. Describing sex is.

> Gershon Legman (1917-), *Love and Death: A Study in Censorship* (1949)

It is legally impossible to rape a woman wearing skin-tight jeans since such a garment cannot be removed without the victim's active co-operation.

> Italian Court of Cassation on acquitting a 45-year-old driving instructor of raping his eighteen-year-old pupil, reported in *The Times*, 12 February 1999

Criminals are admired by their fellows in the following order in the hierarchy of crime:
(1) desperadoes and hold-up men for their violence;
(2) cat-burglars for their skill and daring;
(3) confidence tricksters for their clever cunning.

> Traditional, quoted by P.G. Osborn in *Questions on Jurisprudence* (1961)

… Like the story of the man who sent a letter to the IRS saying: Enclosed is a cheque for $1000. I cheated on my taxes last year, and I can't sleep at night. P.S. If I still can't sleep, I'll send you the rest I owe you.

> Ronald Reagan (1911-), US President, remark at
> Senate campaign rally, 18 September 1986

The reason I prefer criminal to corporate law is that when you walk into a criminal trial you know at once who the bad guys are.

> Sanford Schulman, US criminal
> attorney (1990)

A brewer called Graham Judge whose award-winning ales included Solicitors' Ruin and Grey Wig was jailed for nine months for tax and duty evasion. He failed to pay nearly £140,000 beer tax and excise duty for 2½ years, Warwick Crown Court was told.

> *The Times*, 18 August 1999

PUNISHMENT

The generality of men are naturally apt to be swayed by fear rather than reverence, and to refrain from evil rather because of the punishment that it brings than because of its own foulness.

> Aristotle (384-322 BC)

Let him who sins when drunk, be punished when sober.

> Anon.

And where th' offence is, let the great axe fall.

> William Shakespeare (1564-1616),
> *Hamlet* 4.5 (1600-1)

Use every man after his desert and who shall 'scape whipping?

> William Shakespeare (1564-1616),
> *Hamlet* 2.2 (1600-1)

> I oft have heard of Lydford Law,
> How in the morn they hang and draw
> And sit in judgement after.

… [this] was reported of a judge of the Stannery at Lydford in Devon, who having hanged a felon in the forenoon, sat in judgement on him in the afternoon.

> Sir Thomas Browne (1605-82),
> *Lydford Journey* (1644)

> He that takes what isn't his'n
> When he's cotched will go to prison.

> If you this precious volume bone
> Jack Ketch will get you for his own.

> Warning scribbled on flyleaf of old school book,
> traditional in public schools; Jack Ketch was
> a hangman from 1663 till his death in 1686

Depend upon it, Sir, when a man knows he is to be hanged in a fortnight, it concentrates his mind wonderfully.

> Samuel Johnson (1709-84), remark on 19 September
> 1777 alluding to the forthcoming execution of
> Dr Dodd, reported by James Boswell,
> *Life of Samuel Johnson* (1791)

Here lies Will Smith – and, what's something rarish,
He was born, bred, and hanged, all in the same parish.

> Epitaph

All punishment is mischief: all punishment in itself is evil.
> Jeremy Bentham (1748-1832), *An Introduction to the Principles of Morals and Legislation* (1789)

Aye, it's cauld in here, prisoner, but we'll nae keep ye cauld much longer. We'll be sending ye to a fine, warm place.
> Anon. Scottish judge

[Judge to prisoner who was defending himself stoutly]: Aye, ye're a clever chiel, I can see that, but a hangin' will dae ye guid.'
> Scottish hanging judges (traditional)

Here [in Paris] they hang a man first, and hold the trial later.
> Molière (1622-73), *Monsieur de Pourceaugnac* (1670)

Men are not hanged for stealing horses, but that horses may not be stolen.
> George Savile, 1st Marquis of Halifax (1633-95), *Of Punishment: Political, Moral and Miscellaneous Reflections* (1750)

This morning we condemned three men to death. Two of them definitely deserved it.
> Sebastien Roch Nicholas-Chamfort (1741-94)

From his brimstone bed at break of day,
  A walking the Devil is gone,
To look at his snug little farm the Earth,
  And see how his stock went on.

He saw a lawyer killing a viper
    On a dunghill beside his stable,
'Oh – oh,' quoth he, for it put him in mind
    Of the story of Cain and Abel.

He saw a turnkey in a trice
    Handcuff a troublesome blade –
'Nimbly,' quoth he, 'do the fingers move
    If a man be but used to his trade.'

He saw the same turnkey unfettering a man
    With but little expedition,
And he laughed, for he thought of the long debates
    On the Slave Trade Abolition.

As he went through Cold-Bath Fields he looked
    At a solitary cell –
And the Devil was pleased, for it gave him a hint
    For improving the prisons of Hell.

> Robert Southey (1774-1843) and
> Samuel Taylor Coleridge (1772-1834),
> 'The Devil's Thoughts' (1799)

Inscription
for the Door of the Cell in Newgate,
where Mrs Brownrigg, the 'Prentice-cide,
was confined previous to her execution.

For one long term, or e'er her trial came,
Here Brownrigg lingered. Often have these cells
Echoed her blasphemies, as with shrill voice
She screamed for fresh Geneva. Not to her
Did the blithe fields of Tothill, or thy street,
St Giles, its fair varieties expand;

Till at the last, in slow-drawn cart she went
To execution. Dost thou ask her crime?
SHE WHIPPED TWO FEMALE 'PRENTICES TO DEATH,
AND HID THEM IN THE COAL-HOLE. For her mind
Shaped strictest plans of discipline. Sage schemes!
Such as Lycurgus* taught, when at the shrine
Of the Orthyan goddess he bade flog
The little Spartans; such as erst chastised
Our Milton, when at college. For this act
Did Brownrigg swing. Harsh laws! But time shall come
When France shall reign, and laws be all repealed!

> George Canning (1770-1827) and John
> Hookham Frere (1769-1846). Elisabeth
> Brownrigg was hanged at Tyburn,
> 14 September 1767. Her skeleton
> was for many years displayed
> in a niche at the Old Bailey

If you make the criminal code sanguinary, juries will not convict. If the law is too mild, private vengeance comes in.

> Ralph Waldo Emerson (1803-82),
> 'Compensation' in *Essays*
> (1841)

Punishment tames man, but does not make him better.

> Friedrich Nietzsche (1844-1900),
> *Genealogy of Morals* (1887)

My object all sublime
I shall achieve in time,
To let the punishment fit the crime,
The punishment fit the crime.

* Lycurgus was the lawgiver and founder of the Spartan constitution.

And make each prisoner pent
Unwillingly represent
A source of innocent merriment,
Of innocent merriment.
> W.S. Gilbert (1836-1911),
> *The Mikado* (1885)

Are you going to hang him anyhow – and try him afterwards?
> Mark Twain (1835-1910),
> *Innocents at Home*
> (1872)

The Law of England is a very strange one; it cannot compel anyone to tell the truth … But what the Law can do is give you seven years for not telling the truth.
> Lord Darling (1849-1936),
> English judge

'To my mind,' observed the Chairman of the Bench of Magistrates cheerfully, 'the *only* difficulty that presents itself in this otherwise very clear case is, how we can possibly make it sufficiently hot for the incorrigible rogue and hardened ruffian whom we see cowering in the dock before us. Let me see; he has been found guilty, on the clearest evidence, first, of stealing a valuable motor-car; secondly, of driving to the public danger; and, thirdly, of gross impertinence to the rural police. Mr Clerk, will you tell us, please, what is the very stiffest penalty we can impose for each of these offences? Without, of course, giving the prisoner the benefit of the doubt, because there isn't any.'

The Clerk scratched his nose with his pen. 'Some people would consider,' he observed, 'that stealing the motor-car was the worst offence, and so it is. But cheeking the police undoubtedly carries the severest penalty; and so it ought. Supposing you were to say twelve months for the theft, which is mild; and three years for the furious driving, which is lenient; and fifteen years for the cheek, which was pretty bad sort of cheek, judging by what we've heard from the witness-box, even if you only believe one-tenth part of what you have heard, and I never believe more myself – those figures, if added together correctly, tot up to nineteen years –'

'First rate!' said the Chairman.

'– so you had better make it a round twenty years and be on the safe side,' concluded the Clerk.

'An excellent suggestion!' said the Chairman approvingly. 'Prisoner! Pull yourself together and try to stand upright. It's going to be twenty years for you this time. And mind, if you ever appear before us again, upon any charge whatsoever, we shall have to deal with you very seriously!'

> Kenneth Grahame (1859-1932),
> *The Wind in the Willows*
> (1908)

I do not now believe that any one of the hundreds of executions I carried out has in any way acted as a deterrent against future murder.

> Albert Pierrepoint (1905-92), chief hangman
> in the UK from 1946-56, quoted in his
> obituary in *The Times*

When my grandfather was 21, a boy of nine who had set fire to a house was hanged at Chelmsford. In a previous year, a little way back, a boy of seven and his sister of eleven were hanged at Lyne.

> Lord Gardiner (1900-90), speech in
> the House of Lords against the
> death penalty which led
> to its abolition (1965)

If you want to know who your friends are, get yourself a jail sentence.

> Charles Bukowski (1920-),
> *Notes of a Dirty Old Man*
> (1969)

I don't think everyone can be cured by kindness, it would be surprising if I did after 44 years in magistrates' courts. What I do think is that nobody can be educated by being beaten, which is a different proposition.

> Lady Wootton (1897-1988),
> *Observer*, 1974

The question for judges and magistrates sentencing someone on a first appearance is this: as the chances are four to one that the offender will never come back, is there any point in imposing a custodial sentence unless not to do so would be an affront to justice having regard to the seriousness of the offence?

> Sir Frederick Lawton, *Guardian
> Gazette*, 28 October 1998

From the bench said the senile Judge Percival,
'Young man, Counsel says you'll get worse if I'll
   Send you to gaol,
   So I'll put you on bail.'
Now wasn't Judge Percival merciful?

> Anon.

What, still alive at twenty-two
A clean upstanding lad like you?
Sure, if your throat 'tis hard to slit,
Slit your girl's, and swing for it.

Like enough, you won't be glad,
When they come to hang you, lad:
But bacon's not the only thing
That's cured by hanging from a string.

So, when the spilt ink of the night
Spreads o'er the blotting pad of light,
Lads whose job is still to do
Shall whet their knives, and think of you.

> Hugh Kingsmill, 'Hanging', a parody of
> A.E. Housman, quoted in *Parodies:
> An Anthology* (1960)

PRISONS

Newgate is a dismal prison ... a place of calamity ... a habitation of misery, a confused chaos ... a bottomless pit of violence, a Tower of Babel where all are speakers and no hearers.

> *A Complete History of the Lives and
> Robberies of the Most Notorious
> Highway-Men* (1719)

May God preserve the City of London, and make this place a terror to evil doers.

> Inscription on the foundation stone of Holloway
> prison, 26 September 1849; the old building
> was demolished in 1976 but the foundation
> stone is preserved in the new prison

Under a government which imprisons any unjustly, the true place for a just man is also a prison ... the only house in a slave state in which a free man can abide with honour.

> Henry David Thoreau (1817-62),
> *Civil Disobedience* (1849)

The vilest deeds like poison weeds
Bloom well in prison air.
...

All that we know who lie in gaol
Is that the wall is strong;
And that each day is like a year,
A year whose days are long.

> Oscar Wilde (1854-1900), *The Ballad of*
> *Reading Gaol* (1898)

Prison is a Socialist's paradise, where equality prevails, everything is supplied and competition is eliminated.

> Elbert Hubbard (1856-1915),
> *Contemplations* (1902)

The rusty key creaked in the lock, the great door clanged behind them; and Toad was a helpless prisoner in the remotest dungeon of the best-guarded keep of the stoutest castle in all the length and breadth of Merry England.
...

'Now tell the truth; what were you in prison for?' asked the engine driver.

'It was nothing very much,' said poor Toad, colouring deeply. 'I only borrowed a motor-car while the owners were at lunch; they had no need of it at the time. I didn't mean to steal it, really; but people – especially magistrates – take such harsh views of thoughtless and high-spirited actions.'

> Kenneth Grahame (1859-1932),
> *The Wind in the Willows* (1908)

Anyone who has been to an English public school will always feel comparatively at home in prison. It is people brought up in the gay intimacy of the slums who find prison so soul-destroying.

> Evelyn Waugh (1903-66),
> *Decline and Fall* (1928)

Probably the only place where a man can feel really secure is in a maximum security prison, except for the imminent threat of release.

> Germaine Greer (1939-), *The Female Eunuch* (1970)

Prison is like being in hospital without the fear of pain or in the army without fear of war.

> Lord Kagan (1915-95), who was deprived of his knighthood but whose peerage could not be annulled; on release from prison he returned to the House of Lords

The only thing I really mind about going to prison is the thought of Lord Longford visiting me.

> Richard Ingrams (1937-), editor of *Private Eye*, on the prospect of going to gaol in 1976

Banging up a drug offender in prison is like locking an alcoholic up in a brewery.

> Jim Wallace, Scottish Liberal Democrat leader, Quote of the Day in *The Times*, 21 April 1999

POLICE

A Bow Street Ballad
(By a Gentleman of the Force)

My trembling And amost refewses
> To write the charge which SIR JOHN swore
Of which the COUNTESS he ecuses,
> Her daughter and her son-in-lore.

Crime and Punishment

My Mews quite blushes as she sings of
    The fatle charge which I now quote:
He says Miss took his two best rings off,
    And pawned 'em for a tenpun note.

'Is this the child of honest parince,
    To make a way with folks' best things?
Is this, pray, like the wives of BARRINS,
    To go and prig a gentleman's rings?'

Thus thought SIR JOHN, by anger wrought on,
    And to rewenge his injured cause,
He brought them up to Mr Broughton,
    Last Vensday veek as ever waws.

If guiltless, how she have been slanderd!
    If guilty, wengeance will not fail;
Meanwhile, the lady is remanderd
    And gev three hundred pounds in bail.

William Makepeace Thackeray
(1811-63)

When constabulary duty's to be done,
A policeman's lot is not a happy one.

W.S. Gilbert (1836-1911), *The
Pirates of Penzance* (1879)

The terrorist and the policeman both come from the same
basket.

Joseph Conrad (1857-1924),
The Secret Agent (1907)

I'm not *against* the police; I'm just afraid of them.
Alfred Hitchcock (1899-1980)

[Corrupt police chief]: 'Major Strasser has been shot. Round up the usual suspects.'

> Julius and Philip Epstein and Howard
> Koch, *Casablanca* (1942)

He's not Robeson. Let him go. That's not the American way. ... in this country we don't lynch the wrong nigger.

> US patrolman restraining a lynch mob beating a black
> man in the belief that he was Paul Robeson's son.
> Quoted on TV by Paul Robeson Junior, who
> claimed he had stood by unrecognised

There is plenty of law at the end of a nightstick.

> Grover Whalen (1886-1962),
> US government official

Far more university graduates are becoming criminals every year than are becoming policemen.

> Sir Philip Goodhart (1925-)

It's not the people who are in prison who worry me. It's the people who aren't.

> Earl of Arran (1938-), *The New York Times* (1962)

It has been suggested that the recent dictatorship on the continent ought to be a warning against the establishment of a strong, centrally-controlled police force here. I believe that the lesson is the exact opposite. The danger in a democracy does not lie in a central police that is too strong, but in local police forces that are too weak. It was the private gangs of the Fascists and of the Nazis that enabled Mussolini and Hitler to establish their dictatorships.

> Arthur Goodhart (1891-1978), Professor of Law
> at Oxford, in a separate memorandum of
> dissent from the Royal Commission
> on the Police (1962)

Militant demonstrations require policemen as an essential part of their ritual, to be sworn at, mocked and hated and convenient substitutes for the government.

> Ben Whitaker (1934-), *The Police* (1964)

I have never seen a situation so dismal that a policeman couldn't make it worse.

> Brendan Behan (1923-64), Irish
> writer, twice imprisoned

Reading isn't an occupation we encourage among police officers. We try to keep paperwork down to a minimum.
...
Policemen, like red squirrels, must be protected.

> Joe Orton (1933-67), *Loot* (1967)

Are you going to come quietly or do I have to use ear-plugs?
...
Policemen are numbered in case they get lost.

> Spike Milligan (1918-), *The Last Goon
> Show of All*, Boxing Day 1972

Is there racism in the police force? Yes, there is. Is that racism more than a few bad apples? Yes, it is.

> Sir Paul Condon, Commissioner of the Metropolitan
> Police, commenting on police failure properly to
> investigate the murder of black teenager
> Stephen Lawrence, *The Times*,
> 2 February 1999

A police force's register for officers to declare membership of secret societies has attracted only one signature.

> *The Times*, 30 March 1999

How long, I wonder, before the Criminal Cases Review Commission seeks an inquiry into whether Cain really did kill Abel?

> Diana Waller, commenting on the belated exposé
> of the police cover-up of evidence in the A6
> murder for which Hanratty was hanged
> in 1962, *The Times*, 1 April 1999

I wanted to be a policeman but I had parents.

> Graffito in lift at Croydon
> Magistrates court

Do not ask for bail as a refusal often offends.

> Graffito on wall at Tottenham
> Magistrates Court

The police are always brilliant when they are against you, invariably hopeless when they are on your side.

> Anon.

WILLS

'Leave all the rest to me', engraving by Robert Seymour, *c.* 1830
(Mary Evans Picture Library).

Wills

Wills are among the oldest documents of civilisation. One of the earliest was found in Egypt in the ruined Middle Kingdom city of Lahun and is dated around 1850 BC. Written in cursive hieratic script on papyrus, it bequeaths the deceased's property to his widow and then to his children.

Another papyrus will, held in Oxford by the Ashmolean Museum, dates from 1200 BC. In it, an elderly woman disinherits those of her children who failed to care for her in her widowhood.

But wills in hieroglyphic writing on the stone walls of tombs are even older. One testamentary inscription on the wall of a tomb chamber in Teħna near Minya in Egypt goes back to 2400 BC.

In 348 BC Plato left two farms and four slaves to his son Adimantes 'to whom I also bequeath my chattels listed by Demetrius'.

Wills are usually written on paper, but this is not essential. During the Dark Ages they were sometimes inscribed on bark. More recently one wag wrote his in indelible ink on an eggshell. Another used an old Christmas card. A man once found a will spelled out on the rung of a stepladder borrowed from a neighbour. When the ladder was returned, a Los Angeles judge admitted it to probate.

While in hospital (also in Los Angeles) the doddering Mr Hazeltine took a shine to his two nurses and insisted on leaving each $10,000. No paper could be found so one of the nurses wrote out his will on her underwear. On his death it was proved by his great niece who inherited the lot. The nurses got nothing because they had signed as witnesses. The rule is that no witness may benefit under the terms of the will.

The longest testamentary disposition ever was made by a Mrs Cook who died in 1925. Containing no less than 95,940 words, it consisted of four gilt-edged volumes. One of the briefest was written in his pay-book by a soldier on active service: 'All to Mum.' A serving soldier or sailor may even make a will by word of mouth.

Mutilated wills have been patched up and admitted to probate. An Irish will gnawed by rats, another torn to pieces by an old lady in a state of confusion, a will that went down with a ship, all have been held valid.

Sometimes missing wills which cannot be found have been held effective. One Lord Chancellor, Lord St Leonards, spent the last four years of his life adding codicils to his will which disinherited his grandson. When he finally died in 1875 at the age of 94 all had vanished from his locked bureau. Was his grandson the culprit? We shall never know, but if he had destroyed them all, it availed him not a jot because the court allowed the daughter of Lord St Leonards to recite the text of the will from memory.

The legal rule is that 'a will speaks from death' but this must not be taken too literally. Dictating onto a recording machine will not do. Even a video-tape is of no effect unless accompanied by writing. One man donned a shroud and addressed the camera from his coffin but was nevertheless declared intestate.

Only once has a testator returned from beyond the grave to assist in the interpretation of his will. He appeared before the then Master of the Rolls, Sir Andrew Porter (1837-1919). Sir Andrew was a man who could never bear to be interrupted and it boded ill to anyone who had the temerity to try. He began to give his judgement on the construction of a rather complicated will:

'Now I am perfectly convinced that the testator intended his farm to go to his nephew James,' he declared.

'Indeed he did not, my lord,' came a faint voice from the rear of the court.

'Bring that man forward at once,' roared the judge.

A scrawny, ill-clad man was escorted by the constable to the well of the court.

'How dare you speak while I am giving judgement? Who do you think you are?' bellowed Porter.

'If your lordship pleases, I am the testator, and I never intended James to have the farm,' came the unexpected answer.

It transpired that what the testator claimed was true. Years before, he had emigrated to Australia from his native Ireland and had never troubled to write home. The presumption was that he was dead, and his next of kin began to quarrel over the farm until the dispute finally came before the court.

Another farmer presented his solicitor with the problem of drawing up a will giving each of his two sons an exact half of his land. The sons were always quarrelling and he did not wish the division of the farm to give rise to dissension after his death. His solicitor drafted numerous wills, but none was satisfactory to the testator.

On his death bed he was presented with an elaborately worded document which the solicitor proposed to witness jointly with his young articled clerk. A lengthy argument ensued, during which the articled clerk sat in the corner and pencilled out a clause to be inserted in the will as follows:

'Let my farm be divided equally between my two sons. Let the elder make the division. Let the younger choose his half first.'

The testator smiled and signed it without hesitation.

A lawyer who retired and left his practice to his newly qualified son, was invited to a celebratory supper the following year. 'You must congratulate me,' said the jubilant young lawyer. 'I have succeeded in settling that disputed will case that I came across in the strong room.'

'You idiot,' exploded his father, 'I intended that dispute to keep you in fees until you retired yourself.'

Jarndyce v. *Jarndyce*

The raw afternoon is rawest, and the dense fog is densest, and the muddy streets are muddiest, near that leaden-headed old obstruction, appropriate ornament for the threshold of a leaden-headed old corporation: Temple Bar. And hard by Temple Bar, in Lincoln's Inn Hall, at the very heart of the fog, sits the Lord High Chancellor in his High Court of Chancery.

Never can there come fog too thick, never can there come mud and mire too deep, to assort with the groping and floundering condition which this High Court of Chancery, most pestilent of hoary sinners, holds, this day, in the sight of heaven and earth.

On such an afternoon, if ever, the Lord High Chancellor ought to be sitting here – as here he is – with a foggy glory round his head, softly fenced in with crimson cloth and curtains, addressed by a large advocate with great whiskers, a little voice, and an interminable brief, and outwardly directing his contemplation to the lantern in the roof, where he can see nothing but fog. On such an afternoon, some score of members of the High Court of Chancery bar ought to be – as here they are – mistily engaged in one of the ten thousand stages of an endless cause, tripping one another up on slippery precedents, groping knee-deep in technicalities, run-

ning their goat-hair and horse-hair warded heads
against walls of words, and making a pretence of equity
with serious faces, as players might. On such an afternoon, the various solicitors in the cause, some two or
three of whom have inherited it from their fathers, who
made a fortune by it, ought to be — as are they not? —
ranged in a line, in a long matted well (but you might
look in vain for Truth at the bottom of it), between the
Registrar's red table and the silk gowns, with bills,
cross-bills, answers, rejoinders, injunctions, affidavits,
issues, references to masters, masters' reports, moun-
tains of costly nonsense, piled before them. Well may
the court be dim, with wasting candles here and there;
well may the fog hang heavy in it, as if it would never
get out; well may the stained glass windows lose their
colour, and admit no light of day into the place; well
may the uninitiated from the streets, who peep in
through the glass panes in the door, be deterred from
entrance by its owlish aspect, and by the drawl lan-
guidly echoing to the roof from the padded dais where
the Lord High Chancellor looks into the lantern that has
no light in it, and where the attendant wigs are all stuck
in a fog bank! This is the Court of Chancery; which has
its decaying houses and its blighted lands in every shire;
which has its worn-out lunatic in every madhouse, and
its dead in every churchyard; which has its ruined
suitor, with his slipshod heels and threadbare dress,
borrowing and begging through the round of every
man's acquaintance; which gives to monied might, the
means abundantly of wearying out the right; which so
exhausts finances, patience, courage, hope; so over-
throws the brain and breaks the heart; that there is not
an honourable man among its practitioners who would
not give — who does not often give — the warning,

'Suffer any wrong that can be done you, rather than come here!'

Charles Dickens (1812-70),
Bleak House (1853)

The case of *Jarndyce* v. *Jarndyce*, although fictional, was not entirely an exaggeration. In real life we find the will of a man who died in 1882, fought over for the next eighty years. Its interpretation involved no less than twelve major court battles, ultimately concluded in 1962. The lawyers' fees of all the claimants came out of the trust funds, which were very nearly swallowed up in the process.

TESTAMENTARY DISPOSITIONS

A son can bear with composure the death of his father, but the
loss of his inheritance can drive him to despair.

> Niccolo Machiavelli (1469-1527),
> *The Prince* (1517)

I owe much; I have nothing; the rest I leave to the poor.

> Will of François Rabelais
> (*c.* 1494-1553)

To God my soule I do bequeathe, because it is his owen,
My body to be layd in grave, where to my friends best
    knowen;
Executors I will none make, thereby great stryfe may grow,
Because the goods that I shall leave wyll not pay all I owe.

> William Hunnis, Elizabeth I's Chapel
> Master, the earliest known
> verse will

Let's choose executors, and talk of wills.

> William Shakespeare (1564-1616),
> *Richard II* 3.2 (1595-6)

> To my dear wife,
> My joy and life,
> I freely now do give her
>   My whole estate
>   With all my plate
> Being just about to leave her.

This is my store,
I have no more,
I heartily do give it;
   My days are spun,
   My life is done,
And so I think to leave it.

John Winstanley (?1678-1750),
'A Last Will and Testament'

This fifth day of May,
Being airy and gay,
To hyp not inclined,
But of vigorous mind,
And my body in health,
I'll dispose of my wealth
…
I do therefore enjoin,
And strictly command,
As witness my hand,
That nought I have got,
Be brought to hotch-pot;
And I give and devise,
Much as in me lies,
To the son of my mother,
My own dear brother,
To have and to hold
All my silver and gold,
As th'affectionate pledges
Of his brother, John Hedges.

John Hedges of Hanover Square
(1737)

This is my last will,
I insist on it still,
So sneer on and welcome,
And e'en laugh your fill.
I, William Hickington,
Poet, of Pocklington,
Do give and bequeath
As free as I breathe
To thee, Mary Jarum,
The queen of my harem,
My cash and my cattle,
With every chattel,
To have and to hold,
Come heat or come cold,
Sans hindrance or strife,
Though thou art not my wife;
As witness my hand,
Just here as I stand,
The twelve day of July,
In the year seventy.
        Signed, William Hickington

William Hickington of
Pocklington (1770)

A Lawyer being sick and extream ill
Was moved by his Friends to make his Will,
Which he soon did, gave all the Wealth he had
To frantick Persons, lunatick and mad;
And to his Friends this Reason did reveal
(That they might see with Equity he'd deal):
From Madmen's Hands I did my Wealth receive,
Therefore that Wealth to Madmen's Hands I'll leave.

Benjamin Franklin (1706-90), *Poor
Richard's Almanack* (1734)

An unforgiving eye, and a damned disinheriting countenance!
Richard Brinsley Sheridan (1751-1816),
The School for Scandal (1777)

The King of France's Picture set with Four Hundred and
Eight Diamonds, I give to my Daughter Sarah Bache request-
ing however that she would not form any of those Diamonds
into Ornaments either for herself or Daughters and thereby
introduce or countenance the expensive vain and useless
Fashion of wearing Jewels in this Country.
Will of Benjamin Franklin
(1706-90), 17 July 1788

I give and bequeath
(When I'm laid underneath)
To my two loving sisters most dear
The whole of my store,
Were it twice as much more,
Which God's goodness has granted me here.

And that none may prevent
This my will and intent,
Or occasion the least of law racket,
With a solemn appeal,
I confirm, sign, and seal
This the true act and deed of Will Jacket.
Will proved at Doctor's Commons,
17 July 1789

To employ an attorney I ne'er was inclined,
They are pests to society, sharks of mankind.
To avoid that base tribe my own will I now draw,
May I ever escape coming under their paw. ...

To my loving, kind sister I give and bequeath,
For her tender regard, when this world I shall leave,
If she choose to accept it, my rump-bone may take,
And tip it with silver, a whistle to make.

Will of William Ruffell,
18 March 1803

I therefore give to my dear Wife
All my Estates, to keep for life,
Real and Personal, Profits, Rents,
Messuages, Lands, and Tenements;
After her death, I give the whole
Unto my Children, one and all,
To take as 'Tenants in Common' do,
Not as 'Joint Tenants', 'Per mie – per tout'.

And now, my Wife, my hopes I fix
On thee, my Sole Executrix –
My truest, best, and to the end
My faithful Partner, 'Crown', and Friend.

This Will was published, sealed and sign'd,
By the Testator, in his right mind,
In presence of us, who, at his request,
Have written our names these facts to attest.

John Cooper Grocott,
26 January 1835

What you leave at your death, let it be without controversy;
else the lawyers will be your heirs.

Selleck Osborn (1782-1826),
US journalist and poet

The art of will-making chiefly consists in baffling the importunity of expectation.

> William Hazlitt (1778-1830),
> 'On Will-Making',
> *Table Talk* (1821-22)

God bless you, Gentlemen! Learn to give
Money to colleges while you live.
Don't be silly and think you'll try
To bother the colleges, when you die,
With codicil this and codicil that,
That Knowledge may starve while Law grows fat?
For there was never pitcher that wouldn't spill,
And there's always a flaw in a donkey's will!

> Oliver Wendell Holmes, Sr (1809-94),
> 'Parson Turell's Legacy' (1858)

My will is that my sons should receive solid and useful education, and that no portion of their time be devoted to the study of abstract science. I greatly desire that they may possess a thorough knowledge of the English language, with a good knowledge of the Latin language. I request that they be instructed in the Holy Scriptures, and next to these that they be rendered thoroughly in a knowledge of geography and history. I wish my sons to be taught an entire contempt for novels and light reading, as well as for the morals and manners of those with whom they may be associated or instructed.

> Will of Sam Houston (1793-1863),
> political leader

When you have told anyone that you have left him a legacy, the only decent thing is to die at once.

> Attributed to Samuel Butler
> (1835-1902)

Wills

Ye lawyers who live upon litigants' fees
And who need a good many to live at your ease,
Grave or gay, wise or witty, whate'er your degree,
Plain stuff or Queen's Counsel, take counsel of me:
When a festive occasion your spirit unbends,
You should never forget the profession's best friends;
So we'll send round the wine, and a light bumper fill
To the jolly testator who makes his own Will.
A lawyer intending to frame the thing ill,
Couldn't match the testator who makes his own will,
And the law, when defied, will avenge itself still
On the man and the woman who make their own will.

> Lord Charles Neaves (1800-76), 'The Jolly
> Testator Who Makes His Own Will' (1869)

No customer brings so much grist to the mill
As the wealthy old woman who makes her own will.

> Attributed to Lord Charles Neaves (1800-76)

When it comes to divide an estate, the politest men quarrel.

> Ralph Waldo Emerson (1803-82),
> Journal (1863)

Michael Henchard's Will

That Elizabeth-Jane Farfrae be not told of my death, or made
to grieve on account of me.
& that I be not bury'd in consecrated ground.
& that no sexton be asked to toll the bell.
& that nobody is wished to see my dead body.
& that no murners walk behind me at my funeral.
& that no flours be planted on my grave.
& that no man remember me.
To this I put my name.

> Thomas Hardy (1840-1928), *The Mayor
> of Casterbridge* (1886)

If a man can't forge his own will, whose will can he forge?
W.S. Gilbert (1836-1911),
Ruddigore (1887)

I've often had to notice that a man'll sometimes do the foolishest thing or the meanest thing in his hull life after he's dead.
Edward Noyes Westcott (1846-98),
David Harum (1898)

Doubtless the contesting of wills is a nuisance, generally speaking, the contestant devoid of moral worth and the verdict unrighteous; but as long as some testators really are daft, or subject to interested suasion, or wantonly sinful, all should be denied the power to stifle dissent by fining the luckless dissenter. The dead have too much to say in this world, at the best, and it is tyranny for them to stand at the door of the temple of justice to drive away the suitors that they themselves have made.
Ambrose Bierce (1842-1914), 'Some Features of the Law' in *Collected Works* (1911)

Bequeath, *v.t.* To generously give to another that which can no longer be denied to *somebody*.
Ambrose Bierce (1842-1914), *The Enlarged Devil's Dictionary* (1967)

A man died leaving a large estate and many sorrowful relations who claimed it. After some years, when all but one had judgement given against them, that one was awarded the estate, which he asked his Attorney to have appraised.
 'There is nothing to appraise,' said the Attorney, pocketing his last fee.
 'Then,' said the Successful Claimant, 'what good has all this litigation done me?'

'You have been a good client to me,' the Attorney replied, gathering up his books and papers, 'but I must say you betray a surprising ignorance of the purpose of litigation.'

Ambrose Bierce (1842-1914), *Fantastic Fables*
in *Collected Works* (1911)

You cannot live without the lawyers, and certainly you cannot die without them.

Joseph H. Choate (1832-1917), speech
on 'The Bench and the Bar',
New York, 13 May 1879

If you wait till you are dead ... you get credit for the *intention*, and the lawyers get the money. The stomachs of the lawyers of this land are distended to utter discomfort with the elee-mosynary architecture that they have swallowed. In all this world there is no joy to the joy a lawyer feels when he sees a good-hearted inconsiderate person erecting a free library or a town hall or a hospital in his will. He smiles the smile that only he knows how to smile, and goes into training for the anaconda act.

Mark Twain (1835-1910), speech at Fairhaven,
Massachusetts, 22 February 1894

In a Victorian novel [H. Rider Haggard, *Mr Meeson's Will* (1894)] a short will ('I leave my property to Eustace Meeson') was tattooed on the back of a young lady, together with the necessary signatures; and after a probate action she was duly admitted to probate. The susceptibilities of the day were happily not shocked by any anatomical discussion whether the signatures to the will satisfied the statutory requirement of appearing 'at the foot or end thereof'. At the hearing the will gave evidence of due execution; and although she was en-gaged to the sole beneficiary, she was not married to him, and so no question arose whether, *qua* will, she had been revoked or invalidated by marriage to a beneficiary.

> R.E. Megarry (1910-), *A Second*
> *Miscellany-at-Law* (1973)

'... I would beg you – for the last time, probably – to step round to the village as quickly as possible – even now it may be too late – and fetch the doctor ... And by the way – while you are about it – I *hate* to give you the additional trouble, but I happen to remember that you will pass the door – would you mind at the same time asking the lawyer to step up? It would be a convenience to me, and there are moments – perhaps I should say there is a moment – when one must face disagreeable tasks, at whatever cost to exhausted nature!'

> Kenneth Grahame (1859-1932), *The Wind in*
> *the Willows* (1908) (Toad pretends to be
> fatally ill so that he can make his escape)

There are few grave legal questions involved in a poor estate.

> Ed Howe (1853-1937), US journalist

The only authentic evidence which we have of the survival of life after death is the ability of the judges to read the intention of the testator long after he has been buried.

> Judge Frederick E. Crane (1869-1947),
> *New York State Bar Bulletin* (1931)

If it wasn't for Wills, Lawyers would have to go to work at an essential employment. There is only one way you can beat a Lawyer in a death case. That is to die with nothing. Then you can't get a Lawyer within ten miles of your house.

> Will Rogers (William Penn Adair) (1879-1935),
> 'Well, All I Know is What I Read in
> the Papers', 3 May 1925

Nature has no cure for this sort of madness, though I have known a legacy from a rich relative work wonders.

> F.E. Smith (1872-1930), commenting
> on Communism in *Law, Life
> and Letters* (1927)

We have the highest authority for believing that the meek can inherit the earth; though I have never found any particular corroboration of this aphorism in the records of Somerset House.

> F.E. Smith (1872-1930) (Somerset
> House used to contain the
> Probate Registry)

Just as a mad person cannot make any will, so a sane person cannot make a mad will.

> James Avon Clyde (1863-1944), Scottish
> Lord President of the Court of Sessions,
> in *MacKintosh's Judicial Factor* v.
> *Lord Advocate* (1935)

The cello is not one of my favourite instruments. It has such a lugubrious sound, like someone reading a will.

> Attributed to Irene Thomas (1920-),
> English broadcaster

The testator made his will by the expedient which so many testators adopt of buying a sixpenny or shilling form and filling it in. [He then] signed the will and no doubt thought he had done a good day's work, as, for the legal profession, he had.

> Mr Justice Harman (1894-1970) in the
> Chancery Division of the
> High Court (1951)

I shudder to think that in the hereafter I shall have to meet those testators whose wishes on earth have been frustrated by my judgements.

> Attributed to Sir Harry Trelawny Eve
> (1856-1940), Judge of Chancery
> Division of the High Court

> I think that I shall never see
> A simple perpetuity;
> A comprehensible bequest;
> Devises where remainders vest;
> A clause whose words are plain as day
> And mean precisely what they say;
>
> A case where dying men refrain
> From making lawyers share their pain,
> If wills are made by fools like me,
> Not even God can take a fee!

> 'Kill Joycemer' (pseudonym), 'Forests',
> *Harvard Law Record*, 3 March 1960

Before I die, I shall leave a will, because if you want something done, sentimentality is effective.

> John Cage (1912-92), *Silence* (1961)

Sonny: Being of sound mind and body, and all that shit ... To my darling wife Leon whom I love as no man has loved another man in all eternity, I leave $2,700 from my $10,000 life insurance policy, to be used for your sex change operation. If there is money left over it is to go to you on the first anniversary of my death, at my grave. I expect you to be a real woman then, and your life full.

> Frank Pierson (1925-), *Dog Day
> Afternoon* (1975)

Two sheepdogs in New Zealand have missed out on a
£400,000 inheritance after their eccentric owner's will was
rewritten by court order. The sum set aside – NZ$1 million –
was totally unjustifiable 'even for the most aristocratically
raised dogs', said Auckland High Court Judge, Dame Silvia
Cartwright.

Evening Standard, 19 March 1999

The Testament kicks off with a literal splat, as elderly billion-
aire Troy Phelan, the tenth richest man in the US, signs a will
in favour of and in front of his rapacious ex-wives, several
children, their lawyers and mental health experts. But as soon
as they leave, he whips out his own handwritten version, signs
it and throws himself off the fourteenth floor of his office
building. The second will leaves everything to an illegitimate
daughter nobody knew of.

Review of *The Testament* by John
Grisham, *Law Society's Gazette*,
24 March 1999

The Law Society was quick to point out the need for properly
drafted wills in a story about a pair who lost a £200,000
inheritance because of their uncle's badly written home-made
will.

Daily Mail, 31 March 1999

A man persuaded his mother-in-law to dress up in a wig and
pretend to be a wealthy spinster to have a £1.8 million will
changed in their favour. Annie Kay, 87, the wheelchair-bound
heiress, died eight days after the bogus will was signed by
Annette Russill, 65, who had put on make-up to age herself
20 years in order to fool a solicitor into drawing up the will.

The Times, 27 July 1999

The solicitor, by Kenny Meadows, *Heads of the People*, 1840
(Mary Evans Picture Library).

Index of Authors

Diary of a Man in Despair
Friedrich Reck-Malleczewen £6.99 Paperback 0 7156 3100 4

A forgotten literary masterpiece by a Prussian aristocrat whose fascinating journal and indictment of Hitler's regime, written between 1936 and 1944, has astonished and delighted readers and critics alike.

'very, very rarely one comes across a book so remarkable and so unexpectedly convincing that it deserves more to be quoted than to be reviewed ...I beg you to read this bitterly courageous book'   Frederic Raphael, *The Sunday Times*

'a vivid and extremely personal evocation of the Nazi era – a small masterpiece'   Ben Rogers, *Financial Times*

'an indisputable humanist masterpiece'
                                   Walter Ellis, *The Times*

Cleopatra's Wedding Present
Travels through Syria
Robert Tewdwr Moss   £6.99 Paperback   0 7156 3099 7

Robert Tewdwr Moss describes his travel experiences with rare charm and aplomb.

'it would be hard to find a more archly entertaining, slyly informative, or poignant travel book than this'
                                   Philip Hoare, *Independent*

'Tewdwr Moss's intense, evocative account of his travels through Syria is a perfect book of its kind. Its author demonstrates intelligence, curiosity, humour, compassion, and commendable powers of observation: everything that is required of a travel writer'
                        Lucretia Stewart, *Times Literary Supplement*

The Way of Hermes

Translated by Clement Salaman, Dorine van Oyen, William D. Wharton, Jean-Pierre Mahé   £6.99 Paperback 0 7156 3093 8

The *Corpus Hermeticum* is a collection of short philosophical treatises, a powerful fusion of Greek and Egyptian thought, written in Greek in Alexandria between the first and third centuries AD. They are still read as inspirational spiritual writings today.

These translations of Hermetic writings and aphorisms provide both general reader and scholar with new English versions, based on reliable texts and faithful to the spirit and beauty of the original.

One Woman's War

Eve-Ann Prentice   £6.99 Paperback   0 7156 3104 7

A personal account of the war in the Balkans by a senior *Times* journalist, hailed by Harold Pinter as 'a powerful and important book'.

'*One Woman's War*, spurred by the death of the author's Serb interpreter during the Nato bombing of Kosovo, is an unself-conscious, intensely human and exceptionally honest reflection of the past ten years of conflict'

Allan Mallinson, *The Times*

'makes the valid point that the foreign press engaged in dangerous "demonisation" of the Serbs'

Peter Millar, *The Sunday Times*

'in the best tradition of a rare kind of eyewitness war reporting, the sort that is highly readable, but does nothing to make the military theatre an inviting destination'

Elaine Lafferty, *Irish Times*

The Pig: A British History
Julian Wiseman   £6.99 Paperback   0 7156 3092 X

A history of one of Britain's best-loved creatures, including the development of its husbandry.

'elegantly slender … full of delightful pictures of the different breeds. Gripping'
Independent

'brings home to one what splendid creatures pigs are and what a contribution they have made to good living and even to survival'
Lord Blake, *Financial Times*

'a fine and well-told morality tale, whose basic message applies not only to pigs but to all livestock in all ages, the world over'
Colin Tudge, *New Scientist*

The Captain
The Life and Times of Simon Raven
Michael Barber   £6.99 Paperback   0 7156 3138 1

With an updated prologue, this tremendously well-received biography of the late Simon Raven, one of Britain's most idiosyncratic and talented characters, is published for the first time in mass market paperback.

'this biography is a minor masterpiece'
Evening Standard

'hugely entertaining and scrumptiously readable'
The Times

'scandalously enjoyable'
Independent

'Michael Barber has played a real Captain's innings in this often hilarious biography of Simon Raven'
Jilly Cooper

On Beauty and Being Just
Elaine Scarry   £6.99 Paperback   0 7156 3134 9

An inspirational and extremely lucid philosophical critique on the interpretation of beauty.

'a lucid, passionate and cultivated book'   *The Tablet*

'with exemplary clarity, Elaine Scarry argues that admiring the beautiful is nothing to be ashamed of; that on the contrary beauty fosters the spirit of justice. A brave and timely book'
J.M. Coetzee

Horace: A Life
Peter Levi   £6.99 Paperback   0 7156 3136 5

The first comprehensive biography for 40 years of the life of the great Roman poet.

'a fine example of an old-fashioned literary form: the book by well-informed and enthusiastic amateur, talking to the reader about a poet he has loved for many years'   *The Spectator*

'as usual with a book by Peter Levi, the pages scintillate with rare details'   *Independent on Sunday*

'engrossing'   *Daily Telegraph*

The Uncollected Dorothy Parker
Edited by Stuart Y Silverstein   £6.99 Pbk   0 7156 2937 9

122 forgotten pieces displaying the raw talent and dexterity of America's most renowned cynic. Here is the distinctive wit, irony and precision that continues to attract succeeding generations of writers.

'this volume is a great event'   *Daily Mail*

'adds up to an essential collection'   *Time Out*

'unputdownable ... Silverstein's 69-page introduction is as good a biography as I've read of Dorothy'
Sparkle Hayter, *The Express*

A Short Walk Down Fleet Street
From Beaverbrook to Boycott
Alan Watkins   £6.99 Paperback   0 7156 3143 8

'entertaining and enlightening … Watkins plays Aubrey to the many remarkable personalities who populated old Fleet Street, defining this lost world through a series of splendid pen portraits'   *Sunday Telegraph*

'this short book is the finest account of journalism I have ever read. Literate members of the public should buy it because it is the wittiest book of the year. Undergraduate students of media studies should buy it without fail, for there is more practical information in it than in a hundred lectures …'
                                                                        Literary Review

'I chuckled over every page of this splendid book, the genius of which lies in the detail … '   *Independent on Sunday*

'a hilarious read'
                    Robert Blake, *Daily Telegraph* Books of the Year

'*A Short Walk Down Fleet Street* … is an incomparable portrait of a particular era and way of life, and is impossible to recommend too highly'   *Sunday Express*

'The Law is a Ass'
An Illustrated Anthology of Legal Quotations
Compiled & Edited by Ronald Irving £6.99 Pbk 0 7156 3142 X

This entertaining compendium contains many witty, cynical and sometimes profound observations, sayings and anecdotes about the law, lawyers, courts, justice, crime and punishment, libel and wills.

'Ronald Irving's book is a treasure house of wit, wisdom and anecdote wholly new to me, woven together with comment and narrative drawn from his own wide practical experience and his apparently limitless erudition'   Lord Nolan

An Intelligent Person's Guide to Ethics

Mary Warnock £6.99 Paperback 0 7156 3089 X

'one of the best guides to ethics available'

Ray Monk, *Sunday Telegraph*

'this admirable book fully lives up to its title'

Robert Grant, *The Times*

An Intelligent Person's Guide to History

John Vincent £6.99 Paperback 0 7156 3090 3

'not only is Vincent one of the great historians of 19th-century British politics, he is also that rarest of things in academic history: a witty prose stylist'

Niall Ferguson, *Daily Telegraph*

An Intelligent Person's Guide to Dickens

Michael Slater £6.99 Paperback 0 7156 3088 1

'Michael Slater has an encyclopaedic knowledge of Dickens's writings' *Times Literary Supplement*

An Intelligent Person's Guide to Modern Ireland

John Waters £6.99 Paperback 0 7156 3091 1

'John Waters skilfully attacks those who decry any sense of nationalism or belittle any aspiration that the two parts of Ireland should be united'

Michael O'Toole, *Irish News* (Belfast)

Boogie-Woogie

Danny Moynihan   £5.99 Paperback   0 7156 3102 0

Much-praised hilarious satire of the incestuous world of New York's contemporary art scene.

'Moynihan's first novel is spectacular stuff'

Harriet Lane, *Observer*

'a filthy corker of a book'   Jilly Cooper

'subversive, darkly funny'   *The Times*

'a highly amusing first novel'   *Tatler*

'witty satire... an excellent first novel'   *Daily Mail*

Intimate Cartographies

Lynne Alexander   £5.99 Paperback   0 7156 3095 4

A beautifully-constructed tale of a mapmaker who comes to terms with loss through the discipline of her work.

'Alexander has chosen the most difficult of subjects, the death of a child. She has treated it with sensitivity and wit, manic levity and the utmost respect, and has created something quite haunting'

Carol Birch, *Independent*

Too Fast To Live

Bidisha   £5.99 Paperback   0 7156 3098 9

A modern-day story of misdirected passions and amoral ambitions in a subversive rewriting of the Arthurian saga.

'Bidisha is clearly a dazzlingly creative writer'

Anthea Lawson, *The Times*

'a dark violent tale that gets under your nails like the London grime it describes'   Francesca Gavin, *Dazed and Confused*

'an inventive addition to the current school of cockney cool'

Independent on Sunday

Charlotte
The Final Journey of Jane Eyre
D.M. Thomas   £5.99 Paperback   0 7156 3094 6

An extraordinary, imaginative deconstruction of Charlotte Brontë's *Jane Eyre*, set partly in modern-day Martinique.

'a wickedly irreverent antidote to earnest study'
Charlotte Cory, *Independent*

'the test of a text like this is whether you can put it down. I couldn't. I hurtled on, gripped by the simplest desire any reader ever has. I wanted to find out what happened'
Patricia Duncker, *New Statesman*

Never Trust A Rabbit
Jeremy Dyson   £5.99 Paperback   0 7156 3097 0

Twelve enchantingly surreal stories, recently serialised on BBC Radio Four, by Jeremy Dyson, one of *The League of Gentlemen*.

'*Never Trust a Rabbit* is ...expertly told and structured, being filled with such utterly surreal and fantastic twists and turns as one might expect of a member of BBC2's *The League of Gentlemen*'
Dominic Bradbury, *Times Metro*

'a stunning debut. His stories nestle in the little chink between Roald Dahl and Borges'
Adam Mars-Jones, *The Observer*

Layer Cake

J.J. Connolly   £5.99 Paperback   0 7156 3096 2

The critically-acclaimed contemporary gangland thriller set in London's underworld, described by Bruce Reynolds as 'the best crime novel I've ever read'.

'*Layer Cake* is a storming piece of work, funny and serious by turns with an abiding sense of conviction'

Guardian

'this year's crime read should be J.J. Connolly's Layer Cake'
Mike Pattenden, *Times Metro*

'mission accomplished. One novel in and Connolly has hit the jackpot'

*****, Uncut

The Lantern Bearers

Ronald Frame   £5.99 Paperback   0 7156 3133 0

WINNER OF THE 2000 SALTIRE BOOK OF THE YEAR AWARD, SCOTLAND'S MOST PRESTIGIOUS LITERARY PRIZE.

As the biographer of a dead composer of the 1960s Neil Pritchard is forced to make a moral decision which risks exposing his involvement in the violent events that took place 35 years earlier on the remote Solway Firth, when he was the composer's final muse.

'exceedingly powerful, laced with impending menace from the opening page'

Scotland on Sunday

'a Master of Suspense to rank alongside the greats'

The Times

'bitingly intelligent'

Independent

Valentine's Day
Women Against Men: Stories of Revenge
Edited by Alice Thomas Ellis £5.99 Paperback 0 7156 3140 3

A brilliant collection of revenge stories by some of the finest contemporary women writers around.

'a sharp anthology, both clever and pointed'

The Times

'this cracking collection of Valentine's Day short stories does not mess around with the soppy stuff. This is a book not about romance, but revenge'

Daily Mail

'a fiery and fun mix which is deeply satisfying to read'

Amazon.co.uk

A Kind of Warfare
Portrait of a Serial Seducer
Deborah Bosley £5.99 Paperback 0 7156 3139 X

A frontline account of the battle of the sexes in which an 'Alfie' for our times is hopelessly addicted to serial seduction and romantic self-absorption, until love hits him and he is hoist by his own petard.

'Deborah Bosley's great achievement is to tread a clear and confident path between the surging purple of her subject matter and the economical, self-deprecating wit with which she writes about it'

Literary Review

ORDER FORM (BLOCK CAPITALS PLEASE)

SURNAME _____ FIRST NAME _____

ADDRESS _____

_____

_____ POSTCODE _____

METHOD OF PAYMENT (PLEASE TICK AS APPROPRIATE)

☐ Invoice to my Grantham Book Services account
☐ By cheque (payable to Duckworth Publishers)
☐ Please send account opening details (trade customers only)
☐ By credit card (Access/ Visa / Mastercard / Amex)

Card no: ☐ ☐ ☐ ☐ ☐ ☐ ☐ ☐ ☐ ☐ ☐ ☐ ☐ ☐ ☐ ☐

Expiry date: __ / __ / __ Authorising Signature: _____

POSTAGE (Private customers) Please note that the following postage and packing charges should be added to your order:

UK deliveries: £3 on orders up to £16; £4 on orders over £16
Export surface: £3.50 for first book + £0.50 for each additional book
Export airmail: £7 for the first book + £2 for each additional book

QTY	ISBN	TITLE	PRICE	TOTAL
____	____	_____	____	____
____	____	_____	____	____
____	____	_____	____	____
____	____	_____	____	____
____	____	_____	____	____
____	____	_____	____	____
____	____	_____	____	____

TOTAL £_____

To: Sales Dept, Duckworth, 61 Frith Street, London W1D 3JL
Tel:+44 (0) 20 7434 4242 Fax: +44 (0) 20 7434 4420
Heidi@duckworth-publishers.co.uk